Published 2000 by Sunningdale Golf Club

© 2000 Sunningdale Golf Club

John Whitfield
is hereby identified as author
of this work in accordance with Section 77
of the Copyright, Designs and Patents Act 1988

ISBN 1 874538 62 X

Distributed in the U.K. by
Old Bakehouse Publications
Church Street
Abertillery
Gwent NP13 1EA
Telephone: 01495 212600 Fax: 01495 216222

Made and Printed in the UK
by J.R. Davies (Printers) Limited

Contents

Foreword   vii

Acknowledgements   viii

Introduction   xi

Chapter One   The Early Years   1

Chapter Two   The First World War   14

Chapter Three   The Inter-War Years
                    and the Second World War   23

Chapter Four   Peace for Half a Century   36

Chapter Five   The Courses   55

Chapter Six   The Ladies   81

Chapter Seven   Golf and the Golfers at Sunningdale   92

Chapter Eight   Epilogue   148

Appendices   1 to 13   156

Photographs of   the Captains' Boards,
                    the Honours Boards
                    and Club Trophies   181

Secretaries of the Club   206

Index   207

Tom Roberts - Founder of the Club

Foreword

There are some golf clubs that have, and will always have, a special aura about them. Sunningdale is undoubtedly one.

All that one would hope to find in the ideal golf club is in abundance at Sunningdale. Two magnificently conditioned courses of superb design and so pleasing to the eye, a clubhouse which provides members and visitors with an unforgettable experience of pampered comfort, accompanied by exceptional food and wine, a staff that anticipates and provides for the members' wishes, no matter how eccentric they may be, a first class professional's shop with friendly and competent instruction on hand, the most knowledgeable caddies in the game and the finest half way house I know.

My own memories of Sunningdale bring in so many of the events and outstanding characters who are remembered in this book. Gerald Micklem, the most respected administrator and authority on golf there has ever been; Jimmy Sheridan, who was and still is the best but most intimidating caddie master I have ever met; Jimmie Watt and Arthur Lees. All of these I am proud to have known and counted as my friends.

The fun and pleasure of competing at Sunningdale in the Foursomes and in the Gold Vase will stay with me for many years to come, as will the memory of maple walnut ice cream after lunch, sausages at the tenth green and a pint of Pimms at the end of the round, seated in a comfortable leather chair.

Over the years, Sunningdale members have played a leading role on the R & A Committees, where they have worked tirelessly to ensure that the game of golf is governed in a way which ensures that, whilst desirable standards are maintained, developments in the game keep pace with contemporary customs and aspirations. These are the very qualities that make Sunningdale the Club it is and of which this book so well reminds us.

Michael Bonallack
Captain, Royal and Ancient Golf Club

Acknowledgements

In undertaking this task I was fortunate in knowing what historical material was available in the records of the Club.

The minute books are complete. There is an almost complete set of Annual Reports. Scrapbooks were kept from the early days up to the First World War, but unfortunately not thereafter. There is a complete record of all Club competitions and matches. The original Suggestion Book is still in use. Major Guy Bennett, a former Secretary (1933-1940) wrote a booklet for members in November, 1962, from which I obtained much useful material concerning the early history and the courses. All these sources being available in the Club made a solid start to the work.

Mr. Bob Warters of Golf Weekly, which now owns the Golf Illustrated title, kindly allowed me to spend some time at their Canary Wharf offices to peruse the splendid set of bound Golf Illustrated volumes, and make notes therefrom. The descriptions of several major golfing events are based on accounts in Golf Illustrated. In particular, Jack White's victory in the 1904 Open Championship, and the Amateur Championship victories of Cyril Tolley and Max Macready. I am most grateful to Mr. Warters and Golf Weekly for this invaluable material.

I thank Dr. George Reid, Senior Bursar of St. John's College, Cambridge, who arranged a meeting for me with the College Archivist, and also for allowing me to see College correspondence with the Club, and other records.

Mr. J.C.A. Minoprio kindly gave me information about the mysterious Gloria Minoprio.

For photographs, the Club's albums were a fruitful source, but thanks are also due to the following:-

Golf Weekly for a number of photographs reproduced from library copies of Golf Illustrated.

Allsport for the photographs of professional players, men and women, in chapters six and seven.

London Illustrated News for permission to print the photograph of members in 1906, taken from the Tatler.

Mr. Struan Wiley for the photograph of Jack White's clubs.

Country Life for the Sunningdale Foursomes photograph.

Mr. K. Atkinson for the photograph of the dinner given by the Club to the Artisans in 1950.

Mr. Charles Dimpfl for the photograph of his father, Dalt Henderson and Bob Foster.

Charles Briscoe Knight for the colour photographs of the golf holes.

Howard and Giles Spencer for the colour photographs of the Founder, the Captains' Boards, the Honours Boards, and the Club Trophies.

Gwilym Davies, Managing Director of Old Bakehouse Publications, for his invaluable advice throughout the preparation of the book, and the setting and printing of it.

I am indebted to Nicholas Royds and Mark Wilson who kindly read the early drafts, and made helpful suggestions.

Stewart Zuill, Secretary of the Club, was supportive at all times, and his assistance was particularly helpful in the final stages of production.

Finally, I must record my most heartfelt thanks to Lucy Delacombe who put the text on the word processor, maintained contact with the printer, and undertook numerous other tasks with cheerful efficiency.

* * *

Introduction

In the spring of 1993 I attended my final meeting of the Club Committee as a trustee. Towards the end of the meeting I remarked that the centenary of the Club in 2000 was approaching, and that I felt it was important there should be a Club History. The suggestion met with general approval, and then someone said, "You've got yourself a job!"

In making the proposal I had not given thought to ways and means, but at that moment I realised this would enable me to continue my long and enjoyable involvement with Club affairs, so I accepted the challenge. I hope what follows will measure up to the task, and will be interesting to read.

At the end of the last century golf clubs were being established in Surrey and Berkshire. The oldest of the Surrey heathland courses is Woking, built in 1893. James Connelly has written an excellent history of that Club - A Temple of Golf - in which he points out that "no golf club can be isolated from what is happening in the local community, and the country as a whole." He refers to certain economic, political and social developments as they affected the Club. That approach impressed me, and I make no apology for attempting to do the same.

The railway, and the station at Sunningdale, and then the appearance of the motor car, had much influence in the early years. Then came two world wars, both of which had a significant impact on the Club. It is fair to say that the prime golfing years at Sunningdale, as with many other leading clubs, were between the wars, and in the decade after the Second World War. Since then the golfing and social scenes have changed dramatically. The huge rewards for those at the top of the professional game have led many talented amateurs to turn professional, after a successful career in the principal amateur events. To reach and maintain the necessary standard demands time-consuming constant practice. In the absence of exceptional talent, ambitious young men today devote their time to work in industry, the City, or the professions. Golf is a social activity.

The early chapters deal with what one might call the administrative history of the Club. The chapter on the courses describes their original layout, and how they have developed over the years. Then comes a chapter on "The Ladies", which illustrates many of the social changes which have taken place in the twentieth century, not only in golf clubs. The golfing achievements of many Club members, and of professionals associated with the Club are described, as well as some of the many major events which have taken place on its courses.

I hope this history faithfully reflects the atmosphere and traditions of Sunningdale which justify its position as a leading Club in the world of golf.

CHAPTER ONE

The Early Years

Oone hundred years ago the first Annual General
Meeting of Sunningdale Golf Club was held at the
Café Monico in London on Thursday, 29th March,
1900. Although the course was not open for play until
September, 1901, the Club was clearly in existence and the year
2000 is appropriate for the celebration of its centenary. This is
an endeavour to trace the history of the Club during its first
hundred years, to record some of the notable events and
personalities associated with it, and to describe how it became
one of the best known inland golf clubs in the world.

The last years of the nineteenth century were years of
unprecedented economic and social change. In a relatively
short space of time there came the motor car, the aeroplane, the
submarine and the wireless. These inventions had profound
effects on the people living in the twentieth century, some
beneficial, others downright harmful when they were applied
to the waging of war. As the Club was being set up, indeed, the
South African war was in progress, and it was not long before
many members lost their lives or were wounded in the
catastrophe of the First World War.

During 1899 two brothers, T.A. and G.A. Roberts built a
house in Sunningdale called "Ridgemount". In one direction it
faced what is now the Ladies' Course, and in the other the
present entrance to the Club. The land on which it was
constructed belonged to St. John's College, Cambridge. The
College owned, and still owns, a large estate in Sunningdale,
which formed part of the Benedictine Nunnery of Broomhall.
When the Nunnery was suppressed by Henry VIII, the
Sunningdale estate was obtained for the College in 1524 by
John Fisher, Bishop of Rochester, and one of the executors of
the Lady Margaret of Beaufort, mother of Henry VII, and
Foundress of the College. This Sunningdale property, until its
development by the Ridgemount Estate Company began,
consisted of three farms: Broomhall Farm, Titlarks Farm and

Stavehall or Broomhall Waste. The rest was heather, gorse and pine trees.

A photograph of "Ridgemount" shows the land around this house and Gordon House very bare and almost treeless. There were no shops near the station, and no Ridgemount Road, merely a bridle path over the property running, as it still does, to Valley End, past the Club cottages, and the 9th green of the New Course.

Ridgemount

Soon after taking up residence, Tom Roberts, known as T.A., approached the College with a view to making a golf course, and to creating leaseholds on the adjoining land for the building of quality houses. By 1899 an agreement had been reached with the College, and a Founders' Committee was formed with the Roberts brothers as promoters. A hundred keen golfers were soon found to subscribe for £100 bonds. A contract was signed with Mr. William Park Junior on 4th December, 1899, for the construction of the course for the price of £3,000. In February, 1900, the first Club Committee was formed and it was resolved that the Club should be a Members' Club.

The first Annual General Meeting was held, as already mentioned, in London in March, 1900. Mr. Hubert H. Longman was elected the first Captain of the Club, Mr. Cecil M. Woodbridge was elected Honorary Treasurer, and as a result of a ballot the following seven members formed the remainder of the Committee: Mr. J. Pritchard, Mr. R. Creasy, Mr. H.C. Clarke, Mr. W.J. Rigden, Mr. P. Barlow, Mr. C. Howard and Mr. C. Lound.

The Committee quickly approved plans for a Clubhouse "to cost with fittings not over £6,000, and a dormy house to be added afterwards at a cost to be decided on later." In July, 1900, the Committee found itself considering estimates varying from £1,700 to £2,500 over their budget figure. A situation familiar to subsequent Committees over the years! The lowest tender of £7,699 was accepted, subject to a meeting of Debenture Holders at the end of July to approve the raising of a further sum of £3,000. Surprisingly, at that meeting there was no quorum, and the meeting had to be abandoned. It was reconvened in August when, with the aid of 35 proxy votes and the seven people present, the necessary resolution was passed. *(Appendix 1.)*

The Committee now had the power to raise the £3,000 by whatever means it saw fit, and an interesting solution was adopted. The builders were asked to allow up to £3,000 of the contract to remain on loan at 6% on security of the Clubhouse and lease, and without any personal liability to the Trustees of the Club. This was agreed, and the contract was signed.

However, by the Spring of 1901 it was evident that the extra £3,000 might not be sufficient to complete the course and Clubhouse. A further meeting was called and approval given to raise the figure to £4,000. *(Appendix 2.)* During the discussion many members said they would rather put up more money than mortgage the Clubhouse to an outside source - the builder. The Committee gave careful consideration to this suggestion, and accordingly in a letter to members in June a revised financial scheme was announced. *(Appendix 3.)*

By early 1901 there were 400 members, a remarkable number, including 100 Debenture Holders; the subscription was five guineas, and the entrance fee five guineas. The course was due to open in the autumn.

The Committee requested T.A. Roberts to approach Jack White with a view to engaging his services as the Club professional. "Remuneration was not to exceed £1 a week, and a cottage on the links". Jack White was then aged 28, and had been professional at several Clubs, including Worlington and Newmarket. He was a brilliant player and frequently took part in challenge matches with other leading players of the day. In due course the Secretary reported that Mr. Roberts had been able to engage Jack White for £40 per annum and a cottage on the links. Thus began his long, and sometimes turbulent, association with the Club.

The Green Committee was empowered "to engage Mr. Hugh MacLean (then a gardener in North Berwick, and known to Willie Park) as foreman of the construction works for three months at 36 shillings a week and a cottage, or 40 shillings a week and no cottage." "Mac" became foreman and remained in the service of the Club till he went into honourable pensionable retirement in 1940.

Another servant of the Club, Bert Chapman, gave more than 60 years service as a greenkeeper. He told a former Secretary, Major Guy Bennett, the story of how he was engaged:

"I used to work for a greengrocer in the village, and one Saturday I wanted to go to the Cup Final with a pal. I asked me boss, and he said 'yer can't go'. But I went. I turned up as usual on the Monday, but he packed me off, and said he didn't want me any more. One day I met a pal and he says to me 'hallo Bert, out of a job?' 'Yes', say I, 'I got the sack.' 'Look 'ere', say 'e, 'they're makin' a golf course or something up on the Common. There's the man who's making it.' And he pointed to a man smoking a big cigar. It was Mr. Willie Park. I went up and said, 'Excuse me, sir, I 'ear they're making a golf course or something up on the Common. Any chance of a job for me?' He say, 'Go on up there and you'll see me foreman, Mr. MacLean, and ask him.' I went along and sees old Mac. 'Are you Mr. MacLean?' say I. 'Yes', he say. 'ave yer got a job for me on this 'ere golf course yer makin'?' 'Can yer dig?' says Mac. 'I can do anything', says I. 'Then carry on', says he. 'And next Tuesday I shall have been here fifty years.'" His wage was 4½d an hour.

Since the formation of the Club the duties of Secretary had been performed by the Hon. Montague Erskine on a part-time basis, but during 1901 it became clear that it was time to make a full-time appointment.

A sub-committee was formed to appoint a Secretary. It received 435 applications, and invited six gentlemen to attend a selection meeting. At the meeting Mr. H.S. Colt was selected as Secretary at a salary of £150 per annum. Mr. Colt was a past Captain of Cambridge University Golf Society. He had designed Rye Golf Links, and had been the first Captain of that Club in 1894.

The thanks of the Committee were recorded for all the work the Hon. Montague Erskine had done for the Club as Secretary pro tem, and he was elected an Honorary Member.

The first meeting of the Committee in the new Clubhouse was held on 20th September, 1901. It was an important meeting at which House, Green and Handicapping Committees were set up, and the duties of the Secretary, Professional, and Steward were considered.

In those days a major problem for members was transport. The motor car was in its infancy and members of the golf clubs springing up around London relied on the railway, and the horse-drawn cab. The Committee, therefore, resolved to send a deputation to meet the General Manager of the London and South Western Railway to discuss the train service from Waterloo and the question of cheap tickets for members and caddies. It was subsequently reported that this approach had

Harry Colt - first full-time secretary of the Club.

The early Clubhouse with horseless carriages parked alongside.

been successful. Special return fares were obtained from numerous stations, and two extra Sunday trains were put on for the Club. The General Manager of the London and South Western Railway was made an Honorary Member.

Apart from transport, there was also the problem of communication. Once at the Club the member was cut off from the outside world. Nevertheless, the Committee decided that the Club could not afford to keep a boy at the station for the delivery of telegrams.

The Green Committee was instructed to draw up Local Rules.

Visitors' green fees were set at one shilling per day if playing with a member. Casual visitors' fees were to be 2/6d per weekday, 5 shillings on Saturdays and Sundays, and 10 shillings for a week.

A limit of 550 was put on the membership, more members having been recruited during the year.

The course was opened for play on Monday, 23 September, 1901. *(Appendix 4.)*

Later that year it was agreed to invite H.R.H. The Duke of Connaught to be President of the Club, an invitation which he accepted some time later and remained President until his death in January, 1942.

By the end of 1901 arrangements had been made for Spring and Autumn Meetings, and the Founders' Singles and Foursomes Tournaments. A sub-committee, which included E. Marshall Hall K.C., was appointed to purchase the Founders' Cups to cost approximately £35, £20 and £20 respectively.

Of passing interest, particularly to American members, is that on 3rd June, 1902, Sergeant George Washington and his wife were appointed Steward and Stewardess.

Also that year the Committee resolved that "the Club does not bind itself to take Electric Light at the present time".

Early in 1903 it was decided to build a hut for refreshments and shelter, close to the 10th green. The cost not to exceed £10.

A subsequent hut on the same site was burnt to the ground in 1992, and its replacement, complete with kitchen and 2 WCs to meet planning and Health and Safety requirements - cost £65,000.

In 1904, what today would be a cause for significant celebration, Jack White, the Club professional, won the Open Championship at Sandwich with a score of 296. No doubt this gave rise to some congratulations in the Club, and indeed members raised a purse for him of over £70, but surprisingly there is no mention of it in the 1904 Committee minutes, nor in the Annual Report at the A.G.M. in 1905.

Different customs and attitudes are also revealed in the Club's Rules and Bye-Laws regarding Lady Visitors:

"Ladies may be introduced by a Member to play on any day except Saturdays, Sundays, competition days and public holidays. The lady visitors must play with the Member introducing them. A match in which a lady is playing must allow an ordinary (sic) two-ball match to pass.

Jack White
- Open Champion 1904

Luncheons are not served to lady visitors, and no lady is allowed inside the Clubhouse until after 4 p.m." *(Appendix 5.)*

Other items of interest in those rules concerned:

Fourballs are not permitted on Saturdays and Sundays between 9 a.m. and 4 p.m.

Parties Scoring. Parties noting down their score may be passed by those who are not, unless there is a competition in progress.

Caddies	One shilling per round of 18 holes
	Sixpence for 9 holes or less.
	Booking fee of one penny per round.

Further Bye-Laws regarding Guests and Temporary Members were made by the Committee to take effect from 1st January, 1905. *(Appendix 6.)*

Towards Christmas, 1904, the Committee appointed some of its members to arrange for a curling pond in front of the Clubhouse at a cost not exceeding £100. It was presumably a

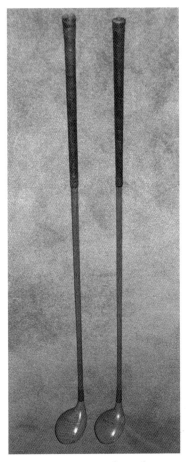

Two examples of
Jack White woods

7

Some Club members in 1906. The names reading from left to right are:
Back row - F.G. Waterer, H.D. Dunbar, F. Dutton, Rowland Hill, E.R. Harvey, C.C. Lingen,
G.J. Hunter.
Middle row - Jack White, A.O. Burton, J. Tindal Atkinson, J. Waterer, D.C. Maddick,
H.H. Longmann, A.J. Stanley, T. Bladworth.
Front row - A.V. Short, S.W. Lawrence, C.O. Webb, J.M. Oldham, P.C. Millard, A.M. Faulkner,
A. Tindal Atkinson, H.C. Clarke, W. Trotter, H.S. Colt, E.A. Hugill, H.A. Trotter, C.C. Clarke
and T.A. Roberts.

Jim O'Brian - Assistant
Professional and
Clubmaker.

hard winter, but it is doubtful whether the pond was ever made as there is no further reference to it.

Little of note occurred in the administration of the Club in the next few years, other than a Committee decision in February, 1907 to build a pigsty and buy some pigs. Also to buy a pony and trap.

In 1909, there are records of several matters. Such as in February, the Secretary reported to the Committee that a letter had been received from a member complaining that Jack White was drunk on the previous Saturday. Other complaints had been made. Apart from being the Club professional, Jack White was a past Open Champion and a noted club maker. One can imagine the quandary of a Club Committee today, but in those days there was no hesitation. The Committee decided that unless Jack White agreed to go into a home for treatment he would be given notice to leave.

On Saturday, 6th March, the Secretary reported that Jack White had gone for three months to a home in Scotland, and it was decided to keep his job open for him for the time being. He returned at the beginning of May.

Having satisfactorily resolved this difficult matter, the minutes record that four days later the Committee decided to lay down 100 dozen bottles of port.

A Club stock book survives, dated March, 1909, and an extract is at *Appendix 7*, giving the cost, and sale prices of various wines, spirits, cigars and so on - a bottle of Scotch sold for 6/8d (33p).

Port was clearly of some importance to many members, one of whom wrote in the Suggestion Book: "3/6d for a small bottle (4 glasses) of very inferior port, undecanted and muddy, is very high. Excellent port can be sold at 6d a glass."

The Reply: "This shall receive immediate attention."

The Professional and Golf Club makers 1905-1910.
Back row, left to right: (1) Herby Givens, (4) Jim O'Brian. Seated: Jack White (centre).

The Committee took an enlightened view of its responsibilities towards the caddies, and during the winter of 1908 evening classes were arranged. In May and November, 1909, letters were sent to all members setting out progress. *(Appendix 8.)*

9

Probably the Club Committee and Trustees when Prince Albert of Schleswig-Holstein (front row, third from left) was Captain in 1910.

One member was clearly not too impressed by all this. He wrote in the Suggestion Book some while later: "I have been charged 2/8d for my caddy today - he was a small boy who did not know one club from another, never kept his eye on the ball, and was apparently about 10 years old. This is an absurd price and should be altered."

Reply: "A mistake was made by the Caddiemaster. Two shillings and sixpence should have been charged. The boy in question is 14 years old, and has only recently come to the Club."

At a meeting on 11th June, 1910, the Committee resolved to start a Working Men's Club, members of it to be allowed to play "before 9 o'clock a.m. or after 6 p.m. except on Saturdays and Sundays, and during Ascot Week." The Captain, His Highness Prince Albert, offered to give a medal for members of the Club to play for.

10

A fortnight later 46 men had sent in their names for membership, and were accepted by the Committee who retained the right to vet members for the new Club. Hugh MacLean, the Head Greenkeeper, was elected Captain with a Committee of seven others.

In July, 1910, the Committee was informed that Jack White had been drinking again. He was sent back to the inebriates home for three months, or such longer period as considered necessary by the doctors there. His job was kept open, but he was told it was his last chance.

Before this incident Jack White had recommended James ('Jimmy') Sheridan as Caddiemaster, who proved to be an outstanding and long-serving servant of the Club.

In December it was resolved to build three pairs of staff cottages near the stables at a cost not to exceed £450 per pair, provided 2½ acres of land could be leased from St. John's College for 99 years. The proposed site gave rise to objections, so the Committee finally decided to take 1½ acres of land on the Chobham Road on a 99-year lease and to proceed with the building of the cottages there.

Club Members with Ladies.

In 1911 the secretarial duties were split, a Mr. K. Greenway being appointed Joint Secretary to deal with the administration of the House, Caddies and General Expenditure, leaving Mr. Colt in charge of all matters to do with the Course and Golf. This arrangement arose as a result of Mr. Colt's increasing commitments as a golf course architect.

As one of his early duties Mr. Greenway was instructed in March, 1911, to obtain another pipe, both of Cockburn's and Dow's 1908 port, and if possible to purchase 50 dozen of Croft's 1896 at 53 shillings per dozen. (A pipe of port is usually 105 gallons or 477 litres, equal to about 636 bottles of 75cl. Thus the order totalled about 1,870 bottles.)

During the Spring of 1911 the Committee received a letter from St. John's College regarding a scheme to build a 9-hole course on Titlarks Farm, and it was resolved to send a circular to members recommending agreement, but asking for a vote on an enclosed card before binding the Club. *(Appendix 9).*

The 1911 Annual Report states there was overwhelming support for the scheme, and that construction of the new 9-hole course was under way. It was named the Sunningdale Heath Golf Club, later to be known as the "chauffeurs' course" or the "nine 'ole". After running into financial difficulties during the 1914-18 war it was taken over by the main Club. In its early days it is recorded that the green fees were almost enough to pay the wages of one man to look after it. A description of its layout is contained in the chapter on the courses.

In July, 1912, the Steward, George Washington, went to Holland without leave, taking with him £46.18.4d - cash received from the previous week, plus £20 petty cash. He returned on 10 July and accounted for all monies in his charge, but refused to explain his unauthorised absence. In view of his long service with the Club, since 1902, he was allowed to tender his resignation, which he duly did.

It is clear from the Minute Book that the two Secretary arrangement did not work out. A special sub-committee was appointed in early March, 1913, to consider the future management of the Club. It reported later that month, recommending that Mr. Greenway be asked to resign, and that Mr. Colt be appointed an adviser for Green matters only at a salary of £100 p.a., being relieved of all other responsibility. Further, that a Secretary be appointed at a salary of £250 p.a., rising over five years to £350 p.a., to take entire charge of the management of the Club. This was all accepted with the exception that the salary should be £250 rising by £25 p.a. to £300.

On these terms Major N.F. Williams was appointed Secretary in April, and at his first Committee meeting was instructed (port again!) to purchase 25 dozen Dow's 1896 at 72 shillings per dozen, and to charge one shilling per glass. He was also to purchase 40 dozen Taylor's 1900 at 46 shillings per dozen.

Another resolution that month was to insure the Clubhouse and course for £1,000 against damage from Suffragettes.

For the next year Club life proceeded without incident, but storm clouds were gathering and culminated in the outbreak of the Great War in 1914.

CHAPTER TWO

The First World War 1914-1918

From 1905 to 1911 there was a running dispute between France and Germany over their respective claims in Morocco. A patched-up settlement in 1906 averted a possible war, but a further crisis broke out in 1911 when French troops occupied Fez, the capital, and the Germans sent a cruiser, the Panther, to Agadir. For some weeks the danger of war again seemed imminent, with the British backing the French, but again a deal was done and war was avoided.

However, from a situation where the majority of British people, particularly the politicians, were broadly well disposed towards the Germans, suspicions of the German government's intentions were now aroused. Anglo-German relations deteriorated, the naval armaments race accelerated, and the seeds of the First World War were sown.

In a rapid sequence of events Austria-Hungary declared war on Serbia on 28 July, 1914; Germany on Russia on 1 August, and on France on 3 August; and Great Britain on Germany on 4 August.

It was generally thought that the war would only last a few months - it would be over by Christmas. A prediction which was hopelessly and tragically wrong, but nevertheless must have had an effect on the thinking of many people in those early days.

The Club Committee, at a meeting in mid-August, decided to make no reduction in the staff or caddie list, but that the Secretary should inform the staff that House wages might have to be reduced and that perhaps only board and lodging could be given. The establishment was to be kept as low as possible. In September it was decided to cancel all remaining 1914 fixtures, and to start a fund for the relief of Belgian refugees. The money subscribed would be devoted to the maintenance of a Belgian family to be quartered in the

Clubhouse. By 1915 a family was living in the Clubhouse and remained there for the duration of the war, their expenses largely paid by the Club.

An offer from a member to pay a bounty of £2 to any member of the staff, or caddie, who enlisted, was accepted.

At this point a saga started which was to continue from time to time throughout the war. His Highness Prince Albert of Schleswig-Holstein had been a member of the Club since its early days. By all accounts he was a popular member, playing to a handicap of 6. He was made an Honorary Member in 1905, and was Captain in 1910. When war broke out he returned to Germany to serve his country. This situation gave rise to the following entry in the Suggestion Book in September, 1914.

"If it is found that any Member of the Club has taken up arms against this country or its Allies, his name be at once removed from the List of Members." (signed by 19 members.)

Prince Albert of Schleswig-Holstein - Captain of the Club 1910.

The Committee clearly realised what was behind the suggestion, and decided to play a dead bat. The Reply was: "This suggestion must stand over for the present."

Immediately under the suggestion was another as follows:

"If it be found that any able-bodied member of this Club has not served his country when called upon in her time of need he be requested to resign forthwith." (Signed by two members).

There was no official reply to this, but someone - possibly the author of the first suggestion - wrote in the Reply column, "Physician heal thyself!"

The next development was in April, 1916, with the following suggestion:

"That Prince Albert's name be erased from the list of Captains of the Club. I believe the feeling in the Club is strongly in favour of this being done."

This was followed by an entry a week later:

"Will the proposer of the above suggestion kindly explain how the erasure of Prince Albert's name can alter the fact that that person was (possibly unfortunately) Captain of the club in the year 1910?"

To which the proposer replied:

"I do not propose to answer conundrums put forward by individual members. As there is apparently still a good deal of friendly feeling towards Germans among the members, I would ask the Committee to ignore my suggestion."

The Committee did just that, as there was no reply to, or comment on, any of these entries.

However, the matter would not rest, and on 30 June, 1918, this suggestion appeared:

"We are surprised to find on our return from Active Service that the name of an alien Prince is still on the board of Captains. We suggest this should be remedied."

The Reply was: "This matter will have the attention of the Committee."

At a Committee meeting on 13 July, 1918, a remarkable decision was made, no doubt after much thought and discussion. It was decided to repaint the Captains' Board, omitting the year 1910!

The final act took place at the A.G.M. in March, 1927, when a motion to restore Prince Albert's name to the Captains' Board, and to invite him to resume his Honorary Membership if he so wished, was carried by a large majority. His name is there today.

Returning to the early days of the war, by the end of 1914 the Committee had decided that troops quartered in the district should have the use of the dining room, the lounge, and the downstairs changing room facilities. The Secretary, now Lt. Colonel Williams, was on active service, and would have his position kept open for him. The Captain, Mr. Norman F. Hunter, would be proposed as Captain for a further year at the 1915 A.G.M. 45 members had resigned, as had 23 "Provisional Members" (those awaiting election to full membership), and 30 new members had been elected.

The outbreak of war had caused much difficulty for the 9-hole Sunningdale Heath Golf Club, and the rent for 1914 was remitted as the Club was not in a position to pay.

In the Spring of 1915 the Board of Agriculture wrote to the club regarding the employment of caddies on farms to relieve the shortage of labour. As a result, the Committee resolved that no caddie over school age, and capable of performing farm work, should be employed.

Furthermore, no unmarried servant of the Club of enlistable age would be employed who had not offered his services to the country.

Following a further letter from the Board it was decided to let the Club's land without payment of rent to suitable applicants for the grazing of sheep, provided the sheep were kept under proper control.

Arrangements were made with the War Hospital at Reading to employ six suitable disabled soldiers to act as caddies at 10 shillings per week each.

In April the problem of Jack White's drinking arose again when it was reported he had been ill due to over-indulgence. It was decided that he must produce a letter every 14 days from his doctor with a statement as to his health, and that the letter must be produced with the utmost regularity.

Jimmy Sheridan, the caddiemaster, was finding difficulty in obtaining the requisite number of caddies, so recruited some local girls, many of whom served as caddies successfully throughout the war.

In July, 1915, the Committee agreed to permit the "Motor" newspaper to bring parties of wounded soldiers to tea in the Clubhouse, and also that the workshops, benches and tools of the Club could be used for the making of periscopes for the trenches. In August some trouble broke out among the staff. Hugh MacLean, Head Greenkeeper, reported that Jack White had interfered with work on the course, and had made accusations of impropriety and bribery against him and Mr. Colt - now acting Secretary - and that he, MacLean was frequently brought home drunk.

After carefully considering evidence from the three men, and two greenkeepers, the Committee decided that the allegations were completely unfounded, that Jack White must apologise unreservedly in writing to the Committee, and that the question of resuming the position of professional - he enlisted in September - "shall abide the result of his military record". In the meantime he was suspended from his post, and it was made clear to him he had not, and never had, anything to do with the management of the course.

In the light of events in the 1990s in the former Yugoslavia, it is of interest that in December 1915, the Committee refused a request for socks and stockings for the Serbian Relief Fund. Nothing much changes in that part of the world.

At the A.G.M. in February, 1916, it was reported that the Captain, Norman Hunter, was missing after the attack on Hooge in June, 1915. He was re-elected Captain, *in absentia,* "in the hope that he would be seen again on the Sunningdale Golf links." Alas, it was not to be, as no further news of him was received.

Norman Hunter and his brother, Mansfield, were both Blues; Norman at Cambridge in 1898, 1900 and 1901, and Mansfield at Oxford in 1897, 1898 and 1900. Diplomatically, they were never paired against one another.

By 1903 Norman's handicap was plus four. He played for Scotland against England, and on a tour of America in August of that year with the Oxford and Cambridge Golfing Society he went round the Chicago Club course at Wheaton, Illinois, in 71. This was four strokes better than the course record set three years earlier by Harry Vardon in the U.S. Open Championship. Clearly, Norman Hunter was some golfer, and his death in June, 1915, whilst serving with the 4th Royal Warwickshire Regiment was a great loss to the Club.

Norman Hunter
Captain of the Club 1914, 1915, 1916 - reported missing June, 1915.

At the same A.G.M. it was noted that the Secretary, Lt. Col. Williams, was now in Flanders in command of the 9th Battalion, Royal Munster Fusiliers. It was not long, however, before the war claimed another victim as in May, 1916, it was reported he had died, presumably from wounds or in battle. The Committee recorded its deep appreciation of his services to the Club.

In February, 1916, Jack White was discharged from the Army and re-engaged as professional on six months probation, subject to instant termination in the event of misconduct.

Jimmy Sheridan was initially rejected for the Army, having flat feet. However, he was not to be deflected from his determination to enlist, and finally succeeded in joining the Royal Artillery in November, 1915, in which he served for three years through to the end of the war. Much of the time he was at the front, and he himself said he was lucky to survive. His wife was permitted to remain in his Club cottage, rent free, for the duration of the war.

In November, 1916, the first professional match in aid of the Red Cross was held. It was an exhibition match, and the players were Harry Vardon, James Braid, J.H. Taylor and Jack White. Further Red Cross days were held in 1917 and 1918 with the same players, who gave their services without payment. Several thousand pounds were raised for the Red Cross and Local War Charities.

In March, 1917, the Committee resolved to continue to allow the grazing of sheep on the course, and to reduce the green staff to three who were to be employed as far as possible for four days a week cultivating the kitchen garden. Consideration was to be given to extending the pig-keeping. The kitchen garden and the pigs were important in helping to overcome wartime food shortages.

In August the Club's mare was sold to Swinley Forest Golf Club for £16, as there was no one to drive her; subject to the right of re-purchase at any time for the sum given. This right was soon exercised, as the mare was re-purchased in October, presumably for £16.

In September, Harry Colt, who had been acting as Secretary since the early days of the war, was offered a post as Assistant

Food Commissioner for the Southern Division of England which, with the Committee's agreement, he accepted. T.A. Roberts took over as Honorary Secretary, E.E. Villiers agreed to assist in supervising the course, and Harry Colt was to be paid an honorarium for his advice as and when needed.

Red Cross Day October 1917. The club raised £1,700 at an auction sale. Left to right: Mrs. Holywell, Carlos Clark, Maude Honeywell and Jessie Carlos Clark.

At the Annual General Meeting in February, 1918, it was noted that the course had been kept in good playing order, and particular attention was drawn to the help given by ladies from time to time, especially Miss Joan Cheney and Miss Molly Griffiths. It was agreed that these two ladies, in recognition of their work on the course, might play the course at any time, and make use of the Clubhouse. They were also each to be given a medal. They were both good players; Miss Griffiths reached the final of the Ladies' Championship in 1920, and later as Mrs. H.M. Heppel she won the 1937 Worplesdon Foursomes with Leonard Crawley.

Other ladies who were working on the course not less than three days a week were to have the following privileges; to play on days other than Saturdays and Sundays without green fee, and on Saturdays and Sundays after 2.45 p.m., without green fee.

One is left to speculate whether this enlightened attitude - for those days - was indeed that, or whether it was hoped by these measures to forestall suffragette damage to the course. One likes to think it was the former.

The liberal attitude of the club was also appreciated in a letter in March, 1918, from Madame Lebert thanking the Club for its hospitality in accommodating this Belgian family for over three years.

In June, 1918, Harry Colt, who had been involved in the running of the Club either as Secretary or adviser to the Green Committee over the past 17 years, was made an Honorary Life Member.

CHAPTER THREE

The Inter-War Years and the Second World War

With the end of the war in 1918, the Club decided that as soon as possible it should appoint a full-time Secretary. From 350 applicants, Mr. F.P. LeMarchand was appointed in March, 1919.

One of the first matters which confronted him was an entry in the Suggestion Book from a member who had clearly not yet accustomed himself to civilian life. It read as follows:

"That a boot parade of the Caddies be held every morning. The condition of some of these children's feet is distracting the players."

The Reply was: "The Committee is of the opinion that this suggestion is not practicable."

Then in May the stables were burned down, and had to be rebuilt. The stables, between the 12th green (Old) and 11th green (New), are now used partly as an equipment store, and partly as a greenkeeping office and greenkeepers' changing and rest room.

Also in that month the Committee decided to invite White, Braid, Vardon and Taylor to play a match for a purse to be raised by the members. The date was fixed for 5th July, and members were invited to make donations not exceeding two guineas. £107 was collected, and in due course distributed as follows: £40 each to White and Braid, £10 each to Vardon and Taylor, and £7 to South Ascot Nursing Home. From this one deduces that White and Braid won, but no details of the match survive in the Club records.

Mr. F. Mansfield Hunter offered the Committee a portrait of his brother, the late Norman Hunter, which was gratefully accepted and now hangs in the Clubhouse.

Sunningdale Heath Golf Club - the nine-hole course - was in financial difficulty throughout the war, and had been supported by the main Club. In July, 1919, the Committee met Mr. F.A. Govett, representing Sunningdale Heath Golf Club, and decided to call a special General Meeting to obtain approval to purchase the lease of that Club for £875. The General Meeting was held in August, and the resolution to purchase the lease was approved unanimously. This step was very important for future plans to build a second 18-hole course for the Club. *(Appendix 10)*.

Membership was starting to recover from the war, and the Committee was advised in mid-1919 that there were 577 members overall, compared with 762 in 1913.

In golfing matters the Club agreed to host the Oxford and Cambridge Universities match in March, 1920.

Lastly in 1919 Field Marshal Earl Haig K.C.V.O. was invited to become an Honorary Life Member, which he was pleased to accept.

1920 was an important year, as a proposal by the Green Committee to extend the 9-hole course to one of 18 holes was circulated to members. James Braid was to be invited to advise on its feasibility. He duly gave his view that it was a practicable proposal, and a special General Meeting was called in July, 1921, "to consider the expediency of enlarging the present 9-hole course to an 18-hole course". This resolution was approved, as also was the purchase of manorial rights for £1,000 from the Earl of Onslow. These rights concerned that part of Chobham Common required for 11 holes of the New Course, the remaining 7 holes being made on the ground of the 9-hole course. It was hoped that play would be possible in the autumn of 1923. Mr. H.S. Colt was to be the architect. In December Mr. Colt outlined his plans for the New Course which he hoped would be ready for sowing by August or September, 1922, at a cost of £8,000 plus fees.

It was decided that the cost of the work would be partially funded by Life Memberships at £150 each.

In 1921 the Committee decided that the Scratch Score of the Old Course would be as follows:

OUT:	5	5	4	3	4	5	5	3	4	=	38
IN:	5	4	5	3	5	4	5	5	5	=	41

Total 79

The Championship Committee of the Royal and Ancient Golf Club of St. Andrews subsequently advised this should be reduced to 78, but there is no record of which hole suffered a reduction, or whether 78 was regarded as an overall total for a scratch player.

The Spring and Autumn Gold Medals in 1921 were won with scores of 75 and 76 respectively.

Much time of the Committee in 1922 was occupied with the construction of the New Course, but one item in the minutes indicates that the war had not diminished members' taste for port. In April the purchase of 100 dozen of 1920 port was sanctioned.

In 1923 it was decided to construct a new 9-hole course on land not used for the New Course. The New Course itself was opened for play on 10th November. The new 9-hole course continued in use until the outbreak of war in 1939, when it was closed, never to be re-opened. Most of the land is now developed for residential housing.

At the end of the year Mr. H.S. Colt was nominated as Captain for 1924. This proved to be a notable year as His Royal Highness, The Prince of Wales, was elected a member, followed a little later by his brother, His Royal Highness, The Duke of York. Both were quite useful players. The Prince of Wales got down to 6, the Duke of York a little higher. They were both Captains of the Club, the Prince in 1930, and the Duke in 1932, and they both subsequently became King.

In June, Sir Gordon Campbell presented the Club with a framed record of its contributions to the Red Cross during the war. The total was £3,138. 19. 7d, which was the best effort of any Golf Club in the Empire.

Also that year Mr. Battell, aged 79, retired after some 20 years running the hut at what was then known as the Ginger Beer Hole (the 10th).

By 1925 Hugh Maclean had been Head Greenkeeper for 25 years, and in recognition of his "Jubilee" his wages were increased from £4 to £5 per week. He was also given £100 and a gold watch.

In September the Committee approved a reduction in the Scratch Score as follows:

OLD	OUT	5	5	4	3	4	5	4	3	4	=	37
	IN	5	4	5	3	5	3	5	4	5	=	39
	Total	76										

NEW	OUT	5	3	5	5	3	5	4	4	5	=	39
	IN	3	5	4	5	3	5	5	3	5	=	38
	Total	77										

However, the major decision taken in 1925 was the agreement to hold the Open Championship Southern Qualifying Round to be played on 16th and 17th June, 1926. This led to the remarkable round of 66 by Bobby Jones on the Old Course which is described in detail in a later chapter. An entry in the Suggestion Book, dated 26th June, 1926, together with the Committee's reply are worth recording, particularly in view of the recently approved scratch score.

"That in view of the fact that the Qualifying Rounds of the Open Championship were played at Sunningdale for the first time in June, 1926, and that Mr. R.T. Jones, who won the Open Championship, beat the record for the course with two rounds of 66 and 68, a tablet to commemorate these facts should be set up in the Clubhouse."

The Reply, dated 10th July, 1926, was as follows:

"The Committee do not agree with this Suggestion. It does not seem to them appropriate to commemorate by a permanent tablet in the Club what, after all, is only an isolated instance of very good scoring."

The 66 round the Old Course has been described many times, and somewhat contrary to the view expressed by the Committee in answering the suggestion, is generally agreed to have been one of the most flawless rounds of golf ever played!

Perhaps the Committee's reply gave rise to some concern in the club, for at the A.G.M. in March, 1927, Bobby Jones was elected an Honorary Member. Happily, also, a framed record of the 66 was made some years later, detailing each shot, and now hangs in the Clubhouse beside a portrait of the player.

In the autumn of 1926 Jack White's retirement at the end of the year was announced. He had been the Club's professional since its beginning, and in the earlier years was undoubtedly one of the best golfers in the country. Unfortunately, his relationship with the Club's authorities had not been an easy one due to his bouts of "over-indulgence." In December, in another relapse, he assaulted his wife in a drunken state causing a severe scalp wound and numerous bruises. In view of his impending resignation at the end of the month no action was taken, but the Committee decided that no "souvenir" should be given. A sad ending to his career.

Jack White at Sandwich in his later years.

There were 72 applicants for the post, and E.F. Scales was appointed.

In January, 1927, the Committee approved the following prices for clubs and repairs to be provided by the new professional:

Gentlemen:	Drivers, Brassies, Spoons	20/-
	Copies	21/-
	Irons, ordinary metal	17/6d
	Irons, rustless	20/-
Ladies:	Drivers, Brassies, Spoons	18/6d
	Copies	19/6d
	Irons, ordinary metal	16/6d
	Irons, rustless	19/-
Repairs:	New head 10/6d; New shaft 9/6d;	
	Specially selected shaft 10/6d;	
	New lead 1/6d; New horn 1/6d;	
	Brass plate 1/6d;	
	New grips proprietary 2/6d;	
	Ordinary 1/6d.	

Before leaving the mid-1920s mention should be made of Agatha Christie, then starting out on her literary career to become a best-selling writer of detective stories. Her husband, Colonel Christie, was a member of Sunningdale and a useful golfer. In 1926 he won the Founders' Singles. In December that year Agatha disappeared for ten days. Underlying this was his infatuation with a younger lady golfer, Nancy Neele.

Mrs. Christie's disappearance became a matter of national fascination. She was, in fact, at a spa in Harrogate under an assumed name. When she reappeared there was a reconciliation, but it did not last and they divorced in 1928. Colonel Christie then married Miss Neele.

There was a sad event in May, 1927, when the recently elected Captain, Mr. J.M. Oldham, died in office. This explains the unusual entry on the Captains' Board of two Captains for 1927.

In June, the first triangular match between the Senior Golfers' Societies of Great Britain, the U.S.A. and Canada took place, and there is an account of it in a later chapter.

In 1928 the name of the Ridgemount Working Men's Club was changed to the Sunningdale Artisans Golf Club.

In June that year the following Suggestion appeared in the Book:

"That a photograph of the Club team (handicap 4 and over), which won the Surrey Golf Union Cup, be taken and hung in a prominent position in the Club."

The Reply was: "The players decline to be photographed."

In 1929 the Committee sought the views of members on a proposal to replace holes 6, 7, 8, 9 and 10 of the New Course with five new holes. The objective was to avoid the "excessive undulations" of the existing holes.

A ballot of members resulted in a majority of two to one against the proposal, and no further action was taken.

His Royal Highness, The Prince of Wales
- Captain of the Club 1930.

The year 1930 was notable for the Club in having H.R.H. the Prince of Wales as Captain. During his term of office it was decided to build four cottages for outdoor staff at a cost of £1,800. Bobby Jones won the Gold Vase, and the Committee finally decided to abandon the 7th Green on the Old Course, as it was sinking and deteriorating.

In 1932 H.R.H. The Duke of York was Captain of the Club. The Committee was concerned about the encroachment of trees, and a programme of removing a number of them, and the undergrowth, was started. The Club tie was approved in that year.

In 1933 the Secretary, Mr. F.P. Le Marchand, died. He had been Secretary since 1919, and by all accounts had been popular and had done the job efficiently and well. Major G.G.M. Bennett was appointed to the post in September.

Also in that year the Scratch Score for the Old Course was reduced from 76 to 74, and the New Course from 77 to 74.

In 1934 the objections of many members to certain holes of the New Course, last raised in 1929, came to the fore again. An E.G.M. was called, and the proposals of the golf architect, Tom Simpson, to replace holes 7, 8, 9 and 10, and make changes to others were approved *nem con*.

In 1935, the reconstructed New Course was opened in October. It was named the Jubilee Course in honour of the King's Jubilee Year. Apart from the four new holes, ten new greens had also been laid.

The minutes that year record that sadly the old Club horse "Ginger" had perforce to be destroyed.

King George V died in January, 1936. In May the Club received a letter from the Keeper of the Privy Purse saying that the new King, Edward VIII, had graciously assented to confer his Patronage on the Club. On Thursday, 10th December, for reasons which are well known, the King signed a Deed of Abdication.

One can only speculate on the nature of what were surely lively discussions in the Club concerning these events. The loss of its royal Patron was, however, soon overcome as in February,

1937, King George VI bestowed his Patronage. It seems clear that both Kings had enjoyed their "off-duty" days playing golf at Sunningdale.

His Royal Highness, The Duke of York - Captain of the Club 1935.

1937 saw the appointment of a new professional, Michael Bingham, as the Committee had decided not to renew the contract of E.F. Scales.

The new holes on the Jubilee Course were not universally popular, and a Suggestion was entered in the Book that the old holes be re-opened. It was not approved, but later in the year it was agreed that play would be permitted on the old holes from time to time, but they would not be re-opened permanently.

In 1938, further alterations were made to the Jubilee Course, and opened for play. However, at the 1939 A.G.M. the argument continued over play on the original New Course holes. A show of hands gave a large majority in favour of the Jubilee Course (that is, the New Course as altered). The Committee decided, in view of the expense of maintaining the original holes as well as the new ones to put the matter to a referendum. This gave a decisive result - 242 votes to 83 - in favour of abandoning the old holes, and this was done.

In July, 1939, an opportunity arose to purchase a portrait of Jimmy Sheridan, painted by Martin Ronaldson, which had been hung in the Royal Academy in 1937, for one hundred guineas. Most of the money was raised by subscription from members, and the portrait hangs in the Members' Bar.

James Sheridan - Caddiemaster 1911 - 1967.
Honorary Member 1956.

There was clearly some discontentment over the running of the Club in 1939, as happens in all Clubs from time to time. A special sub-committee was set up to investigate complaints of matters left undone, or done unsatisfactorily. It submitted its report to the main Committee in July, and recommended pensioning off the Head Greenkeeper, the Steward and his wife, and the clerk in the office. The Secretary was to remain for at least 18 months with new staff. These recommendations were accepted.

In view of the Declaration of War on 3 September, 1939, an Emergency Committee meeting was held that day. It was decided to rescind the proposals for retirement of staff agreed in July. Only the bar would be open in the Clubhouse and a skeleton staff retained, the remainder being given a fortnight's notice. Greenkeeping staff of military age were given a month's notice.

All competitions, matches and visiting societies were cancelled. The courses were to be closed in alternate weeks from Monday to Friday.

With such a swift reaction there was clearly no feeling this time that it would all "be over by Christmas".

By October, Major Bennett, the Secretary, had rejoined the Army, and James Moir took over as Honorary Secretary.

In December it was agreed that Hugh Maclean would retire on 31 January, 1940. Michael Bingham, the professional would supervise work on the courses.

In February, 1940, the Artisans Club offered to maintain the Jubilee Course for the duration of the war, which offer was gratefully accepted.

The Government notified the Club that the Clubhouse was to be requisitioned from 1 October, 1940. A decision was taken to modify and use the Caddies' Canteen as a temporary Clubhouse. "Sunnyside", the Secretary's house, would be used as accommodation for staff and storage, and the Secretary compensated for moving elsewhere. However, as he was by now on active service the problem was not urgent, and in fact he resigned in November.

In May an Exhibition Match took place between Henry Cotton, Michael Bingham, James Braid and Alexander Herd. £508.15.3d. was raised for the Red Cross Fund.

One sunny evening in September Jimmy Sheridan was helping the green staff by mowing the 18th green and the putting green. Unknown to him some German Bombers on their way to bomb the Vickers factory at Weybridge had been intercepted by our fighters, and were dropping their bombs indiscriminately so as to lighten their payloads and increase their chance of escape.

Bombs dropped near the Clubhouse, and Sheridan, who had taken refuge in a bunker, was lucky to escape unharmed. One of the bombs made a large crater on the right of the 18th green, and this was subsequently made into the two bunkers which are now such a feature of the hole, catching many second - or third shots which are fading and slightly off line.

In December, James Moir, the Honorary Secretary since the outbreak of war, was made an Honorary Member.

In 1941, Michael Bingham resigned as professional, and Percy Boomer was appointed in his stead. Percy Boomer was born in Jersey in 1897. He was a five times winner of the French Open, of the Belgian Open in 1922 and 1926, and of the Dutch Open in 1924, 1925 and 1926. He played in the Ryder Cup in 1927, when he was also joint runner-up in the British Open - the year when Bobby Jones won it by 6 strokes. Finally, he won the Italian Open in 1932. At one time before he came to Sunningdale he was professional at St. Cloud, Paris. He was a noted teacher, and wrote a popular book of instruction.

Also in 1941 the New Course was closed for the duration, and rapidly became overgrown. In December, 1942, it was requisitioned by Aldershot District for training purposes. No further reference in the Club minutes to the Jubilee Course is to be found, so henceforward all references are to the New Course.

The picture that emerges, therefore, of the Club during the war years is of troops occupying the Clubhouse, the New Course closed, limited play on the Old Course, and some financial difficulty. Although the Club was on a care and maintenance basis, it was found necessary to request a reduction in the ground rent, to which St. John's College generously agreed.

In the latter part of the war a big review of troops took place on the 1st fairway, inspected by King George VI. There is a story, which may be apocryphal, but has a ring of truth in it. As the King passed the caddiemaster's office, where Jimmy Sheridan was standing, he called, "Good morning, Sheridan". To which Jimmy is said to have replied, "Good Morning, your Majesty. If I may say so, you are making a far better King than you ever did a golfer!"

In 1945 T.A. Roberts died, and many tributes were paid to him as the virtual founder of the Club, and for many subsequent years of work on its behalf. His brother, G.A. Roberts, was appointed to take his place on the Committee.

Also in 1945 James Moir retired; he had done sterling work as Honorary Secretary during the war. George Kirke, a former member, was appointed to take over as Secretary from 1 January, 1946.

The New Course was de-requisitioned from 14 November, 1945 and the Clubhouse from 31 December.

CHAPTER FOUR

Peace for Half a Century

Considerable damage had been done to three holes of the New Course during the military training exercises; in view of this, and the condition of the remainder, it was clear it would be some time before the course could be re-opened.

As a result of an initiative by Brigadier-General A.C. Critchley in 1948, an arrangement was made with the Artisans Club whereby in return for an improvement in their playing rights on the New Course they would supply labour to assist in its re-opening. Thus by autumn 1948 ten holes had been re-opened. A further five were in play by the spring of 1950, but the remaining three holes requiring major work were not ready until October, 1950, when the New Course was formally re-opened.

The Old Course had been maintained as far as was possible, and within a couple of years after the end of the war was ready to be host to major events. In 1948 the Golf Illustrated Gold Vase, the Daily Mail and the Dunlop professional tournaments were all played at the Club.

In 1949 Percy Boomer, the Club professional, who had been ill for some time, died. Arthur Lees, the professional at Dore and Totley Golf Club, Sheffield, was appointed to the post. Arthur, with his inimitable brand of Yorkshire humour, became one of the great characters of the club in the latter half of the century. More will be said about his personality and his golfing achievements in a later chapter.

Although the courses and the Clubhouse were by now recovering from the effects of the war, the finances of the Club were facing the familiar problems which arise when income does not meet expenditure. At a Committee meeting in September, 1949, it was reported that the Club's overdraft of some £5,000 was likely to rise to £8,500 by the year end. It was

Sam King driving at 3rd hole Old Course - Daily Mail Professional Tournament 1948.

decided to call an Extraordinary General Meeting to consider raising subscriptions by four guineas for a Full Member and two guineas for a Junior Member, the then current subscriptions being fourteen guineas and nine guineas respectively; also to consider a possible issue of bonds, and whether the restoration of the New Course should be completed or abandoned.

St. John's College had waived the rent for 1948, and the half-year to 30 June, 1949. The continuing generosity on the part of the College was very much appreciated.

At the E.G.M. in October, a lengthy discussion of the proposals resulted in substantial differences of opinion, and it was agreed to adjourn the meeting for one month. At the adjourned meeting it was agreed to issue bonds to reduce the overdraft, and to the increase in subscriptions. There was a further proposal to admit Lady Members. It had been clear for some time that younger men who could have been suitable candidates for membership were favouring neighbouring Clubs where ladies were admitted, and there was also the additional income the ladies would bring. The admission of Lady Members would thus have a beneficial effect on the Club's finances and membership, quite apart from any other considerations. However, after much argument, it was decided to postpone a decision for one year when the financial position would be reviewed. The proposal to complete the restoration of the New Course was carried *nem con*.

G.L. d'Abo, Captain in 1949, speaking at a dinner given for the Artisans Club in 1950 for their help in renovating the New Course. Henry Longhurst in foreground.

One week after the E.G.M. a Committee meeting was held. Those present were the Captain - G.L. d'Abo - H. Gibson Fleming, T.E. Cunningham, G.A. Roberts, S.G. Sillem, F.S.A. Baker, G.E. Beharrell and the Earl of Lindsay. It was reported that Brigadier General A.C. Critchley, Wing Commander P.B. Lucas and N.J. Smyth had resigned from the Committee.

A stormy discussion took place, with G.E. Beharrell, supported by S.G. Sillem and T.E. Cunningham, taking the view that it was for the Committee to decide subscription rates, and that the E.G.M. decision could be ignored. F.S.A. Baker considered the Committee could not go against the decision of an E.G.M. Lord Lindsay said it was obvious that both the Club and the Committee were split, and that the whole Committee should resign, leaving the members to elect a new Committee. This got no support, so Lord Lindsay thereupon resigned and withdrew.

F.S.A. Baker and H. Gibson Fleming then proposed that the subscription increases agreed at the E.G.M. should go ahead. On a vote, Baker, Fleming and the Captain voted in favour, Beharrell, Cunningham and Sillem against. The Captain used his casting vote to carry the motion. Beharrell and Sillem then resigned and withdrew.

In the following week the Captain resigned, as he had been put in an impossible position, and the Club had a major crisis on its hands.

A Caretaker Committee was formed under the chairmanship of T.E. Cunningham (known as "TEC"), the previous year's Captain, to act until the next A.G.M.

A circular was sent to members *(Appendix 11)* stating that subscriptions would not be raised, a bond issue would be made, and members were invited to make voluntary donations to Club funds. Nominations for the Captain and Committee for 1950 were invited. A postal ballot would be held, and those elected would take office at the A.G.M. in February. There were two nominations for Captain - the only occasion such a procedure has been followed - and 18 nominations for the Committee.

At the 49th A.G.M. T.E. Cunningham was elected Captain with nine Committee members. The meeting agreed that the views of all members should be sought on proposals to rectify the financial situation, and on the admission of Lady Members. The Committee was empowered to take whatever action it deemed fit on consideration of the replies.

Accordingly, having examined the state of the Club's finances, the Committee wrote to members a month later saying it was not possible to run the Club with the present membership without raising subscriptions. Rather than do this, however, they proposed to increase the membership and keep the current rates of subscription. It was suggested that every member should set himself a target of introducing at least one new member.

Instead of the bond issue, a fund for outright gifts would be opened to reduce the bank overdraft which had risen to £11,000.

Finally, a referendum paper was enclosed with detailed proposals for the election of Lady Associate members *(Appendix 12)*. The referendum replies showed a large majority in favour of admitting the ladies, and the proposals were implemented.

The Secretary, G.G. Kirke, retired in May and was made an Honorary Member. It was decided to sell the Secretary's house, "Sunnyside", for £6,500, and the post was offered to, and accepted by, Bernard Drew, then Secretary at Deal (Royal Cinque Ports Golf Club). He agreed to live in the Clubhouse, which was a further help to Club finances.

St. John's College was still foregoing the rent, but with the measures now decided upon the Club resumed payment from Christmas, 1951. As already mentioned, the College had been extremely helpful to the Club during its financial difficulties, and furthermore had contributed £500 towards the restoration of the New Course.

During all this turmoil the following Suggestion appeared in the Book: "It is suggested that the Committee should alter the colours of the Club tie. I suggest many members consider the present tie to be an unworthy symbol of Sunningdale."

The Reply was:

"The Committee consider that as the present colours are so well known it would be a mistake to change them, notwithstanding the significance which has been attached to them in some quarters."

This Reply is a reference to a remark attributed to Henry Longhurst when he was told that the blue and brown striped tie was that of Sunningdale. Any member of more than a few years standing would be able to inform the reader what the remark was!

The Club now entered calmer waters, and in the next few years little of note occurred on the administrative side.

Arthur Lees was the only winner of both his Singles and Foursomes in the 1951 Ryder Cup. The Club gave him a cocktail party and made a presentation.

In 1953 Jim MacLean was appointed Head Greenkeeper, following in his father's footsteps.

1954 was notable for the problems of Sunningdale Ladies Golf Club, which is adjacent to the men's Club on its western side. The Ladies Club was in difficulties, both over administration and greenkeeping, so an arrangement was made on a temporary basis for general supervision to be under the men's Club Secretary and Head Greenkeeper respectively. This also involved the loan of equipment from time to time. No doubt the arrangement led to many outsiders thinking that the Ladies club was a part of Sunningdale Golf Club, but this was never so; the two Clubs are quite separate. "No connection with the firm next door!", but there are many ladies who are members of both Clubs.

Also in 1954 the informal post-war agreement with the Artisans Club was reviewed. In recognition of their help in restoring the New Course their playing rights had been extended, and they had continued to do some greenkeeping work. This work was no longer necessary, apart from some divotting, and after a meeting with the Artisans Committee a limit was imposed on membership, an annual subscription was to be paid to the Club, and starting times were agreed.

In 1956 Jimmy Sheridan, after 45 years as Caddiemaster, was elected an Honorary Member. He retired in 1967, and died in October, 1970. A remarkable servant of the Club for 56 years.

Jimmy Sheridan with members at his Retirement Party.

With members and caddies.

Later that year Arthur Lees was also elected an Honorary Member.

In 1959 the Committee considered a proposal to re-build the Clubhouse. The matter did not proceed, but the suggested method of financing is of interest in that Life Memberships were to be offered. It was assumed that subscriptions would rise to £35 within ten years, and to £50 within twenty-five years. A Life Membership would be offered for £2,000, which would entitle the member to free membership for life, and the right to nominate a relative of the next generation to have similar terms on the member's death. It was reckoned that if a member and his nominee lived for a combined period of fifty years, and the average subscription over this period was £40, this would come to £2,000, ignoring the member's loss of interest on the money.

As the subscription after the next forty, let alone fifty, years was around the £1,000 mark, perhaps it is just as well that this proposal never got any further.

In the 1960s the Committee was giving much consideration to the club's property. The land on which the Old Course was laid out, together with six holes of the New, and the Clubhouse, were subject to six leases from St. John's College. There was a seventh lease covering the eight cottages on the Chobham Road. Twelve holes of the New Course were owned freehold by the Club, the land having been bought from Lord Onslow

42

in 1922 (168 acres) and 1954 (20.5 acres). These holes were numbers 4 to 15, while 1 to 3 and 16 to 18 were on College land.

The problem facing the committee was that the main lease of the Old Course (165 acres) was due to expire in 1970, whilst the remainder had expiry dates ranging from 1980 to 2010. It was clearly desirable to negotiate a new consolidated lease embracing all of these, and an approach was duly made to the College.

However, in 1965 the chance arose to buy the freehold of 193 acres of land adjoining the New Course from the estate of the late Lord Onslow, and in December, 1966, this land was acquired for £1,000.

The Committee then suggested to St. John's that consideration should be given to selling all the Club's freehold land to the College in exchange for a new long lease of the whole area on favourable terms. Negotiations of this kind are by nature somewhat protracted, perhaps fortunately, as a subsequent Committee firmly resolved that the Club would not sell its freehold land. So it was back to the proposed consolidated lease, and after lengthy negotiations, complicated by Government legislation and the necessity for St. John's to obtain the approval of the Minister for Agriculture and Fisheries (!) under the College Estates Act, 1964, a new 60-year lease was signed in December, 1975. This combined all existing leases except that for the Chobham Road staff cottages. The club wished to exclude this as it was entitled to assign the lease, or any part thereof, and this clearly had a significant value.

The lease for the cottages was granted in 1911, and was due to expire in 2010. The first group of four cottages was built in 1911, and the second group of four in 1930. There were no bathrooms, and no electric light, the latter being supplied to the cottages just before the Second World War. Bathrooms were added in 1962, but there was no central heating.

The cottages were cheaply built, and despite improvements did not compare favourably with local authority housing. Due to the absence of central heating, the cottages tended to be damp, and there were frequent complaints from the occupants about condensation. Expenditure on repairs was an increasing cost. Furthermore, it was thought probable that future legislation would entitle an occupant to remain *in situ* should he leave the Club's service, provided he paid a rent that would doubtless be well below the rack rent.

In the light of all these factors, and the growing desire of staff to own their houses, the Committee decided in 1976 to sell the cottage leases. One cottage was vacant, and the lease was sold without difficulty. The freehold of the remainder was then obtained from St. John's, and gradually all were sold, save one which is still in the Club's possession. Most of the cottages were bought by the staff living in them. In 1990 the Club found it necessary to put up a building near the Clubhouse to accommodate young, single, greenkeepers. During the summer months when the green staff have to report for work at an early hour, public transport is not available; rooms in the vicinity are scarce and expensive. Hence the decision to build. The cottages, had they been retained, would not have been suitable for the purpose in mind, and in the circumstances outlined above there is little doubt their sale was justified. The new building - the Gatehouse as it is called - provides four modern bed-sitting rooms with the usual facilities, and a larger room for the housekeeper. Beneath the rooms are storerooms, a garage, a workshop and a wine store.

Having resolved not to sell the Club's freehold to St. John's the Committee turned its attention in 1973 to the recently acquired 193 acres from the Onslow estate. Could it be exploited for the Club's benefit? At a meeting with the Divisional Planning Officer, he suggested that if the club itself wished to use the land for the purpose of golf, an application would probably meet with a favourable response. However, the land was registered Common Land, and thus it would be extremely difficult to prevent the public from straying into areas where there was a risk of being struck by a golf ball. A commercial development would require a clubhouse and carpark which, from a planning point of view, would intrude upon the landscape. Such an application would almost certainly be refused. Residential development would certainly be refused, the land being in the Green Belt.

A soil survey was commissioned, and was distinctly unfavourable, saying that the area was boggy, and the cost of construction would thus be high. Neither the Club's finances, nor the profitability of golf were what they later became, and the Committee decided not to proceed.

The proposition to build a third course was again examined in 1984, and again rejected. In 1987 a group of members once more suggested looking at the possibilities. About this time the Planning Committee of Surrey County Council published a Review of Golf Facilities in Surrey, which stated that golf courses could be an appropriate use for Green Belt land.

However, there was by now a further difficulty. The whole area of the unused Club land had been notified under the Countryside Act 1949 as a Site of Special Scientific Interest, and again under the 1981 Act. The latter imposed even tougher restrictions on what could, and what could not, be done in the area of an S.S.S.I.

Chobham Common, of which the Club's land forms part, has long been known as a site of outstanding botanical and faunal interest. It is a very important national site for invertebrates, particularly ants, bees and wasps, aquatic beetles, flies, butterflies, moths and spiders. It has the largest known spider fauna in Britain - approximately 40% of all British species have been recorded on the Common. Upwards of 80 species of birds breed on Chobham Common, including rare heathland species such as hobby, stonechat and wood-lark. The Dartford warbler is recorded occasionally. The Common is also one of the most important breeding sites in Britain for the nightjar.

In these days of environmental concerns what chance would a golf course planning application have in the face of that information? However, discussions took place with the Nature Conservancy Council - now English Nature - but despite a sympathetic attitude, their statutory duty to protect areas classified as S.S.S.I. could not be overcome. They said they would have to oppose an application to build a golf course as it could not be done without damage to the S.S.S.I. A survey commissioned by the Club from a specialist unit of Liverpool University confirmed that view, and the Committee decided not to pursue the project.

In 1992 the third course yet again was under consideration. Discussions took place with the P.G.A. European Tour who were interested in the possibility of building a championship course on the land, in conjuction with the Club. When not in use by the European Tour, which would be at the most for one month of the year, the course would be a "pay and play" with the profit to be shared between the Club and the Tour on a basis to be agreed.

All the information, discussions and conclusions were gone over again. An Environmental Assessment by the Surrey Wildlife Trust was commissioned by the Tour and submitted to English Nature.

At the end of it all, the last sentence of a letter from the Conservation Officer of English Nature repeated their view "that the nature conservation case for objecting to the development of a further golf course is very strong". The 1994 Club Annual Report makes it clear that in the light of this the project has been shelved, at any rate for the time being.

Going back to 1970, it was clear that the Clubhouse was in need of considerable refurbishment to bring it up to current standards. A detailed survey was undertaken, and a brochure outlining three options with their financial implications was sent to all members with a ballot form. The three options were: to build a new Clubhouse sited between the existing Clubhouse and the 18th green, and extending over the practice putting green; to make a major conversion so that the prime space upstairs would be better used; or to do the minimum renovation work to put the building in good order, and simplify future maintenance, together with some improvements to the changing rooms, bar, professional's shop and caddies' accommodation. The three schemes were estimated to cost £250,000, £150,000 and £50,000 respectively. Although there was some support for a new clubhouse, there was a large majority in favour of the third option of renovation. Accordingly, the work was put in hand and completed in 1972 at a cost of some £58,000.

Eleven years later, in 1983, the Committee put forward a plan for further major improvements. After taking account of comments at the 1984 AGM, a revised plan was adopted. This involved bringing the members' changing room downstairs and putting the visitors' changing room upstairs, as well as creating a new bar upstairs with a view over the courses, now known as the Walker Cup Room. This work also involved changes to the administrative offices. It was completed in 1985 at a cost of some £65,000.

In 1993 and 1994 further upgrading of the entrance hall and the visitors' and ladies' changing rooms was undertaken, thus bringing the Clubhouse up to the standard of a Club of international standing, but without losing its traditional character. In 1999 the Members' Bar was completely refurbished.

In 1974, some excitement was caused at the Club by the murder of Lord Lucan's nanny. Lord Lucan was a member of the Club and was wanted by the police for questioning about the murder. In December, on a gloomy day, two detectives from the Murder Squad turned up to question the staff, and to examine the contents of Lord Lucan's locker; as far as one is aware their visit yielded little in their hunt for the missing peer.

During 1975 the National Police Championships were held at the Club. Every Club administrator has his favourite incident to relate, and the author makes this contribution. Two days before the Championship, the Plastics Industry Golfing Society held its meeting at the Club, and whoever raised their flag let go of the halyard, so the flag with the logo PIGS now rested at the top of the flagpole with no means of getting it down. The Fire Brigade was approached through local authority contacts, and although willing to help, they pointed out that their extending ladder vehicle would ruin the putting green, in which the flag was situated. The flagpole was presented to the Club in 1972 by the ebullient David Wickins, a well-known member and at that time Chairman of British Car Auctions. A call to him brought a typical response, "No problem, leave it to me". In no time at all two men were on the spot, dismantled the pole, removed the flag, and re-erected the pole. Crisis over - thank you, David!

1975 was the 75th anniversary of the founding of the Club. A Dinner with some 200 members and guests, including the Captain of the Royal and Ancient Golf Club as guest of honour, was held in May at the Savoy Hotel in London. An International Anniversary Tournament was held at the end of June, being 36-hole foursomes with one round on each course, with teams from 40 clubs. The event was won by Portmarnock with a score of 151 after a tie with Rye. These celebrations were masterminded by Nicholas Royds with his customary flair.

Arthur Lees retired as professional at the end of 1975. He continued to play a competitive game of golf for many years despite being afflicted with cancer. He died in 1992.

Jimmie Watt, Arthur's long-serving principal assistant also retired in 1975. He lost his right arm in a car accident in 1951, and first played in the World One-Armed Championship at St. Andrews in 1958. He lost in the semi-final, and in 1959 lost in the final, but in 1960 won at Troon against his old friend Alex Wilmott, who had beaten him in 1958. He won at the 19th, the only time he had ever been up, and there had never been more than one hole in it. It was at Troon he last played in the Open Championship before his accident. Jimmie died in 1995.

Jimmie Watt and Jimmy Sheridan.

Arthur Lees was succeeded by Clive Clark, who had been the Club's tournament professional since 1966. Clive had a good record in amateur golf before turning professional in 1965. The peak of this early part of his career was reached in 1965 when he played in the Walker Cup match against the United States at Baltimore. In the vital match he was one down with one to play, and was left with a putt of some 30 feet to win the 18th, which he holed under intense pressure to halve not only his own match, but the entire match with 11 matches each with two halved.

As a professional Clive tied third in the Open Championship at Hoylake in 1967, and later won several tournaments before being selected for the Ryder Cup in 1973.

Clive left the Club in 1984 to pursue his career in television commentating and golf course design. He continues an informal association with the Club.

Keith Maxwell was appointed Club professional at the end of 1984. He had been Head Assistant since 1977. He turned professional in 1973 and from 1975 until he came to Sunningdale, he was Head Assistant at Dumfries and County Golf Club. Keith continues to serve members and visitors with lessons and his well-stocked shop.

When Bernard Drew retired as Secretary in 1960 he was succeeded until 1963 by Commander L.A. Jeffrey OBE, RN, the Assistant Secretary. Colonel Ronnie Yeldham CBE then held the post from 1964 until he retired in 1969. It was a difficult period, when the post-war golf boom was taking off with more golfing societies wanting to play at Sunningdale. There were also more members playing throughout the year, and expecting the courses to be maintained to a high standard all the year round. In addition, inflation was causing significant increases in expenditure and subscriptions.

When Ronnie retired, pending the appointment of a new Secretary, John Whitfield, a member of the Committee, took office as Honorary Secretary from October, 1969. The Committee at that time was much occupied with the proposals for the Clubhouse referred to earlier, and with the renewal of the Club's leases.

On 1st July, 1970, Lawrence Haigh was appointed as Secretary. He served the Club loyally until 1973 when he accepted the post of Secretary at West Sussex Golf Club.

John Whitfield, who had been Captain in 1971, and Honorary Treasurer from January, 1973, accepted the Committee's invitation to become Club Director from 1 May, 1973, with responsibility for all day-to-day administration. During his term of office the Club leases were re-negotiated, the Club's finances and administration were re-organised, and five years of the Colgate European Women's Open Championship took place. In 1978 he resigned due to increasing commitments as a magistrate, and as he was about to become Vice-Chairman of Surrey County Council, and later Chairman.

In March, 1978, Keith Almond, the Secretary of Hexham Golf Club, and a past Captain, was selected as Secretary from numerous applicants. Keith soon settled into the job, and became an invaluable guide and mentor to Captains over the next 13+ years. He took over when the courses had suffered the ravages of two years of drought, the worst being in 1976. With the advice of Jim Arthur, the R & A agronomist, he gradually restored the courses to a high standard. He supervised the installation of the fairway watering system in 1978, and the building of two reservoirs with a capacity of seven million gallons. With the aid of Mervyn Jones as Honorary Treasurer a computerised accounting system was introduced.

Keith Almond was responsible from the Club side for seven professional European Open Championships, and the Walker Cup in 1987, as well as numerous other events. For the Walker Cup he worked with Nicholas Royds, who was Chairman of the Walker Cup Committee, and the Club received many congratulations for its handling of the event. Only the result of the match was a disappointment, the United States winning comfortably.

Keith Almond was a most valuable servant of the Club, and was made an Honorary Member in 1984. He retired in 1991.

For most of the years that John Whitfield and Keith Almond were in office, Cecil Elliott, a member since 1966, was Deputy Secretary, standing in for them when necessary, and responsible with Gerald Micklem for running the Sunningdale Foursomes. Cecil retired in 1989 and was made an Honorary Member. He was a most reliable and helpful member of the team.

Stewart Zuill was appointed Secretary when Keith retired, and took office in July, 1991. He came to Sunningdale from Highgate Golf Club where he had been Secretary for some five years. He has been a scratch golfer in his time, County Champion of Stirlingshire, and with his brother - they are known as the Zulus - has a remarkable record of victories as a member of the Merchiston Castle team in the Halford Hewitt.

He is still in office, but when the time comes he will surely be recorded as a successful holder of that difficult post, Secretary of Sunningdale Golf Club. He was assisted by Christopher Lane as Deputy Secretary from 1991 to 1999.

Jim MacLean, who had been employed by the Club since 1929, retired as Head Greenkeeper at the end of March, 1974, having worked loyally all those years, first under his father, then later in the top job himself.

He was followed by Hugh MacGillivray, who had trained at St. Andrews, and who had the problem of restoring the courses after the mid-70s droughts. He left in 1980 to become Head Greenkeeper at Worthing in Sussex.

Then came Jack McMillan, father of a well-known green-keeping family. Jack did excellent work on the courses during the European Open years, and for the Walker Cup in 1987. He left in 1989 to take up work as a golf course consultant. Bob Bennett followed him, but in 1990 decided to return to Scotland for family reasons. In 1991 Lawson Bingham was appointed Course Manager. Lawson came from Prestwick, and did much to improve and maintain the courses. The Club was fortunate to have his services for some five years before he took a post as Head Greenkeeper at Penina in Portugal.

Jim Maclean
Head Greenkeeper
1953 -1974.

Brian Turner was appointed to the post and took up his duties in early 1996. Brian served his apprenticeship at Sunningdale, moving to Wentworth as an assistant green-keeper, then Course Foreman of the West Course. In 1982 he became Head Greenkeeper at Worplesdon until taking the post at Sunningdale. He is a Sunningdale Artisan, a handicap 1 golfer, Surrey County player, National Artisans Champion seven times, Surrey Artisans Champion twelve times, and Surrey Mid-Age Champion twice.

His uncle is Archie Turner, a Sunningdale Artisan for very many years, a past winner of the Railwaymen's Championship and of the News of the World Artisans Championship, playing off scratch.

Over the years there have been many changes to the Clubhouse staff. One of the Club Stewards after the last war was Mickey Flynn who, apart from running the bar, acted unofficially as a bookie's runner. Temptation to act as bookie himself, unknown to his clients, led to his downfall and departure from the Club. The undesirable practice of using a member of the staff to place bets has now thankfully been stamped out by firm action of the Committee.

Another Club Steward was Sergeant Drummond, lately of the Scots Guards. His sense of humour was not always appreciated by younger members with no service experience, but many older members enjoyed some of his sallies. On one occasion he was approached at the bar by someone who said he had left his money at home, so could he cash a cheque? Drummond asked him if he was a member, to which the reply was, "No, I am afraid not." "Oh, well," said Drummond, "That's all right, then!"

When four Americans came to the Club in a chauffeur-driven "limo" they were obviously determined to have a good day out. At lunchtime, after the odd gin, they called Drummond and ordered four bottles of white wine, four bottles of red, and two bottles of port. Drummond said, "May I ask which two of you gentlemen are not drinking port?"

In 1985 David Lindley came to Sunningdale as Clubhouse Manager from Hallowes Golf Club near Sheffield. He and his wife gave a high standard of service in the Clubhouse which was recognised by a presentation when they retired in August, 1995, and went to live in France. He has been succeeded by Christopher Donovan from the Caledonian Club. He has settled in well and maintains the high standards sought by the members.

Early in 1995 the latest type of computerised till system was installed in the bars, improving financial control and control of stock.

Chris Osborne was second chef in 1975 when Ken Roe, the chef, took a post at short notice with an industrial organisation. Chris was promoted on the spot, and is still with the Club over twenty years later producing good, traditional golf club lunches, as well as dinners for special occasions.

A great deal of work is undertaken in the Club office, which is fully equipped with its computerised accounting system, word processing, photocopier and so on. In January 1993 Lucy Delacombe took over from Lyn Bugler as Stewart Zuill's secretary. Lyn moved to Wales after six years at the Club. In 1995 Lucy was appointed Assistant Secretary.

A most important step was taken in 1975 for the future of the Club when the Committee decided to re-form the cadet section. This was immediately popular, and now has some 70 cadets under the age of 18, mostly sons of members. They have their own competitions and matches, and many are good players. In 1988 James Fletcher, Richard Guest-Gornall and Peter Hale were selected for the 1989 Swift's Tour of the United States. In 1992 Anthony Wall played for England in the Boys' Internationals and won the Surrey Amateur Championship at Wentworth. He has also played for the British Isles against Europe, and in 1995 won the Gold Vase at The Oxfordshire. The majority of cadets become Junior members when they reach the age limit, and it is interesting to see the names of the next generation following their fathers as winners of various Club competitions. Major General Peter Leuchars as Captain in 1975 took the initiative to found this section and thereby ensure a steady flow of younger members to the Club. The late Harry Reeves first took charge of the section, followed by John Wilkinson - schoolmaster and classics scholar by profession, but known to his charges as "Wierdie". Latterly Tony Biggins has devoted much time and energy to the cadets, and has done a splendid job in organising their activities.

In 1992 the Caddiemaster, Fred Scott, died after a number of years at the Club. The position was taken by Vince Reeves, who has settled in well, and Sunningdale still has a large number of senior and junior caddies, in particular at the weekends.

Also in 1992 the Halfway Hut was burnt to the ground; the work, it was thought, of vandals. As mentioned earlier, the re-built hut cost some £65,000, much of the expense being occasioned by the insistence of Local Authority officers that more sophisticated kitchen facilities had to be installed, together with two W.C.s and associated drainage. The latter seemed superfluous to many members, but with the extensive tree thinning and pruning which has been undertaken perhaps more use is being made of them than originally thought. The Hut is situated near the 10th green of both courses, and is a feature of the Club. A wide selection of refreshments is always available throughout the year, with Vernon Collinson and his staff providing a friendly and efficient service.

The Halfway Hut

In the same year the Club was obliged to spend £27,000 on fire precautions in the Clubhouse, despite having been approved by the Surrey Fire Brigade a few years earlier before the county boundary changes took the Club into Berkshire. However, with the Club's registration at risk there was no alternative but to comply.

A second major fire occurred in 1993, when the Club's machinery shed - built in 1988 - was destroyed. The fire was started by static electricity in a tractor, and 95% of all the Club's machinery, and the shed, were destroyed. The total damage was around £400,000, fortunately most of it met by insurance. Although the Club ended up with new machinery, the rolling replacement programme was considerably disrupted.

The Club enters its second century in good heart, and financially sound. If its future members are as well served as they have been by its Committees and officials in the past 100 years, they should have little cause for complaint.

CHAPTER FIVE

The Courses

Willie Park, Junior, was a leading player amongst the golfers of his time. He won the Open Championship at Prestwick in 1887, and again at Musselburgh in 1889, where he was the professional. Later he became known as a golf architect, and was responsible for some fine courses: West Hill, Huntercombe and Sunningdale Old Course all owe their original design to him.

The greens he laid out at Sunningdale were large, perhaps not surprisingly as, according to Bernard Darwin, his long game was erratic, his driving being particularly untrustworthy, but he more than made up for it with his putting. He practised this tirelessly, and Darwin commented that he was perhaps as good a putter as ever lived.

When he came to lay out the Old Course the site was mostly gorse and heather, although there was a large wood through which were cut the 7th to the 10th holes. The area is blessed with sandy soil which is ideal for golf, giving good drainage and tight lies.

In 1900 and 1901 when the course was being constructed the "Haskell" and other rubber-cored balls had not come into use, so the course was laid out for the gutty ball. In the hundred years since then the golf ball has altered beyond recognition; and the use of steel or graphite-shafted clubs, as opposed to hickory, increasingly with metal heads instead of persimmon or laminated wood, has increased the distance the ball is hit. These developments have caused many changes to be made in golf courses. The following account attempts to show how the courses at Sunningdale have altered over the years to meet these challenges.

The Old Course
6323 yards: SSS70

1st hole, 492 yards, par 5
(All yardages are from the white tees.)
The 1st tee was originally more or less on the site of the present 18th green, near the famous Sunningdale oak tree (actually two trees which have grown together). The rough on the right of the fairway came in twenty or thirty yards from its present alignment, thus making the line for the drive more towards the present 17th green. The bunker on the left of the 18th fairway did not then exist. When the New Course was built the tee was moved in 1922 to its present position; part of the gardens of Derry and Sunnyside were acquired and taken in to the right-hand side of the fairway, enabling the right rough to be cut back. This accounts for the different, rather lush texture of the grass near the hedge in that area.

The heather banks on either side of the gap through which one walks to the green, and which are a considerable nuisance to the shorter hitter, marked the corner of a field. If the line of the bank is followed across the 17th fairway, the boundaries of the field can be made out.

The 1st hole shared a large green with the 17th until 1907. It was nearer the heather banks than at present, and the ditch, part of which still exists, ran right across the line of play and had to be carried to reach the green. The bank in front of the green had been lowered, but the ditch was clearly a significant hazard and in 1910 the part guarding the green was filled in, and the green was moved to its present position.

In 1922 a bunker was made on the left-hand side of the green, and in 1928 another, smaller bunker was made in the left slope. This was extended some eight feet to the right and more into the green in 1961; in 1995 the two bunkers were joined to make a large one.

2nd hole, 466 yards, par 4.
The 2nd tee has been pushed back over the years. Bunkers on the right of the fairway, placed to catch a sliced drive with a gutty, were taken out of use in 1960, although lesser players frequently visit the area with a modern ball and club from a tee further back.

A bunker over the road about 150 yards from the green was added in 1928. This often presents a problem for the second shot of the shorter hitter, but rarely troubles the scratch golfer.

The bunker on the left of the green was extended to the right, and more into the green, in 1961. The green slopes from front to back and many a ball runs through leaving a tricky return shot.

3rd hole, 292 yards, par 4
The 3rd hole has been little altered except for a new back tee for major events. A bunker on the left of the green was removed in 1960 and the hollow left with grass and heather.

4th hole, 157 yards, par 3
The 4th green was originally to the left of the present green on the lower ground. The far right tee was the one in use, and the tee shot was virtually blind.

Around 1910 the green was moved to its present position. In most pin placings the bottom of the pin still cannot be seen, and the shot is uphill; a little more club is necessary than seems needed at first sight. Large bunkers guard the front and left of the green, with a smaller one to the right.

5th hole, 407 yards, par 4
When the 4th green was in its original position, the 5th tee was at the top of the hill behind it. The new 4th green made it necessary to move the 5th tee as the new green was in the line of play.

The 5th green was also moved to the right at the same time, thus making the pond much more of a hazard for a poorly hit second shot.

In 1961 the bunker on the right of the fairway from the drive was brought some five yards into the fairway, and another bunker added a little further on. In 1970/71 the pond was enlarged and landscaped. The side nearest the green was revetted with sleepers in 1996.

6th hole, 386 yards, par 4
The main alterations to this hole have been to the bunkering. Until 1961 there were two cross bunkers guarding the green, and a third small one between them some ten yards further on. The latter was known as "Monty's bunker". R.H. de

4th green, 5th & 6th holes, Old Course.

Montmorency, one of the Club's leading players between the wars, could not always carry the cross bunkers with his second shot, but he was so accurate he could play between them. Legend has it that the small bunker was put there to foil him! In 1961 it was removed, and the left-hand bunker filled in with turf and heather. A new bunker was cut just short and left of the green.

7th hole, 393 yards, par 4

The 7th hole was the subject of a major alteration. The drive was played as at present, a blind shot over a large bunker, now disused, in the hill facing the tee. The second shot was played dog-leg left over another large bunker, the outline of which can still be seen, to a green in the hollow - another blind shot.

Alterations to the hole were already being discussed by 1908, but no decision was taken. However, by 1921 the unsatisfactory layout of the hole was finally accepted; also, the green was sinking and deteriorating being low-lying and poorly drained. In 1922 the Committee decided on a new green - the present one - but there was a division of opinion about keeping the old green in play as an alternative. The Committee minutes indicate that this happened for a time, but there is then no further reference to the matter and no doubt the condition of the old green solved the problem without more argument.

8th hole, 168 yards, par 3

The original 8th tee was near the former 7th green. This hole was also subject to criticism, and changes were suggested as early as 1906. When the 7th green was moved the opportunity was taken to re-align the hole and re-shape the green. Since then the hole has been lengthened and the teeing areas enlarged.

The bunkering round the green was extended in 1970, and in 1992 the left-hand greenside bunker was enlarged and brought more into the green, making room for a pathway behind it.

9th hole, 267 yards, par 4

The main changes to this hole are in the bunkering, and in the construction of a two-tier green in 1981.

At first there was only a left-hand bunker protecting the original 10th tee. A bunker on the right was added, leaving a gap of about sixteen yards between the two. When the two-tier green was made, a bunker was put in the face of the upper green. In 1992, a bunker was made on the back left of the lower green to stop balls going on to the 10th tee.

Most of these changes were attempts to make life more difficult for players trying to drive the green. This is well within the capability of the lower handicap player, and certainly a professional would regard the hole as a "pick-up birdie", rather like the 3rd hole. No doubt these holes were not so easy with a gutty ball and a hickory-shafted club.

As the hole can be driven congestion can result during a competition or tournament. Major Bennett, a former Secretary, records that on one occasion during the Golf Illustrated Gold Vase there were no less than nine couples waiting on the tee! Cyril Tolley and his partner were so disgusted at the long wait that they gave up and walked back to the Clubhouse.

Much thought has been given to lengthening the hole, but owing to the configuration of the ground major earthworks and the destruction of trees would be necessary. Even then only a matter of fifteen or twenty yards would be gained, and the big hitters would still have to wait for the green to clear. For the shorter hitter the hole is a challenge, and with the pin on the top tier of the green he is as likely to take five as four.

10th hole Old Course with Halfway Hut.

10th hole, 459 yards, par 4

This hole presents one of the most attractive views on the course. Standing on the tee at the top of the hill, the fairway with bunkers left and right is set out before one. Further on is a bunker in the middle of the fairway which frequently catches the handicap player's second shot. Then with bunkers left and right just short of the green there is the welcome sight of the expensively re-built Halfway Hut behind it.

At some time before the Second World War the bunker in the middle of the fairway was moved nearer the hole. At a later date a new back tee was built, but otherwise there has been little change.

11th hole, 299 yards, par 4

The 11th is widely regarded as one of the classic short par fours. In its original form it appears to have had a large green on the same level as the fairway. In 1910 the Committee decided to make a double plateau green with a hollow between them. The left-hand green had a short life as by 1922 it was no longer in use, and has never been reinstated.

In 1928 a bunker was made in the hollow in the left face of the green.

A ditch runs along the right-hand side of the green, and until 1993 a heather bank and a small grassy hollow lay between the ditch and the edge of the green. In 1993 the heather bank was removed, the hollow was filled in, and the green taken to the edge of the ditch. The effect of this was that a ball running to the right edge of the green could finish in the ditch, instead of leaving a tricky little pitch from the hollow. Whatever the merits of the change, it gave rise to much controversy; it affected the playing of the hole, and was done without following the accepted and sensible procedure of seeking members' views beforehand.

The approach to the 12th green, Old Course.

12th hole, 416 yards, par 4
The green for this hole was at first on the lower ground to the right of the present green; the latter was made in 1911

61

together with the mound in the right face. A bunker on the right of the fairway was added in 1921, but was later taken out of use and a new one made further on, also off the fairway. This was subsequently moved to the left and into the fairway.

Old Course. 13th Green, 2nd and 17th Fairway. Titlarks Hill in background in the early days.

13th hole, 173 yards, par 3

This hole was originally played from a tee beyond the former 12th green, making a blind shot of 260 yards over the hill to a rectangular green. In 1907 the hole was shortened to 160 yards played from the present tee at the top of the hill, thus giving the player a view of the green. The green was enlarged leaving the bunker - much smaller then than now - in the middle of the putting surface. As the alteration, which was unpopular, had been designed by Harry Colt, the bunker became known as "Colt's Po". Later the green was reduced to its present size, and the bunker, no longer in the green, was enlarged.

From the first there was a grassy hollow on the right of the green, but to the left there was a patch of fairway level with the green, leaving the player who hooked his tee shot with a simple chip. In 1970 John Tullis, then Chairman of the Green

13th hole, Old Course.

Committee, proposed making a similar hollow on the left side of the green, thus making a more difficult recovery shot. This was done, and the hollow became known as the "Tully Gully".

14th hole, 475 yards, par 5

There has been little change to this hole other than to the bunkering, and the narrowing of the fairway by allowing quite a large area of rough to grow in on the right.

Two disused bunkers can be seen, one left of the fairway, and one right, level with the right-hand of the oblique line of bunkers crossing the fairway.

15th hole, 222 yards, par 3

The present medal tee is the original tee for this hole. The tee to the left of the 14th green was made in 1918, and enlarged in 1994. A third tee over the ditch to the right of the medal tee is on the Club's freehold land; it was out of use for many years, but was renovated in 1980 to relieve pressure on the main teeing area.

The green was formerly much larger, extending towards the tees, and this accounts for the lushness of the approach.

16th hole, 423 yards, par 4

Apart from lengthening the back tee by some yards, and a narrowing of the fairway by allowing the rough to grow in, this hole is virtually unchanged.

17th Green, 18th hole. Old Course

17th hole, 417 yards, par 4

As mentioned earlier the 17th hole shared a large green with the 1st hole when the course was laid out, but this arrangement soon gave rise to objections, no doubt because of delay caused by players on one hole waiting for others to clear the green. Although the huge double greens of St. Andrews were probably in Willie Park's mind, the area is simply not large enough. In 1907 the 17th green was moved to the ground on the right of the present green, making the hole a right-hand dog-leg. This situation lasted until 1922 when the green was moved again to its present position to make way for the New Course.

18th hole, 411 yards, par 4

In the early years this hole was longer than at present, and was played from a tee near the clump of trees on the left of the 17th fairway. The line was towards the left-hand side of what is now the 18th of the New, thence to a green more or less halfway between the present Old and New 18th greens. The green sloped from back to front, and was guarded by a deep cross bunker, the outline of which can still be seen although it is covered by broom bushes.

In 1922 the hole was completely altered to make way for the New Course. The green was moved to its current position; it was a large one and it had a very wide entrance so any sort of second shot, given the length, would find it. The 1939-45 war greatly improved the hole as the green was reduced in size for reasons of economy, and as mentioned in Chapter 3 the Luftwaffe created two new bunkers, thus making the second shot a much more testing proposition.

Course Records:
Amateur - S.J. Stilwell 65:   Professional - N. Faldo 62
(The Championship Course measures 6619 yards - SSS 72)

The New Course
6443 yards: SSS71

Soon after the end of the First World War the membership figures were recovering rapidly, and transport to the Club was becoming easier. Many members were now coming by motor-car so there was much less reliance on the train; the amount of golf played was increasing, and the Committee was concerned to reduce the pressure on the Old Course.

The lease of the 9-hole course had been purchased in 1919, and as related in Chapter 3 a General Meeting of the Club in 1921 approved the use of such part of that course as necessary, and the purchase of 168 acres of Chobham Common from Lord Onslow, for the making of a new 18-hole course. Mr. Harry Colt was the architect, and the New Course opened for play on 10 November, 1923.

Compared with the Old Course, the New has seen many more changes in its shorter life. In particular, the original holes 6, 7, 8, 9 and 10 were much criticised - mainly by older members - for the amount of climbing involved, and this led to major changes in the mid-1930s. These holes were on the land to the right of the 10th hole, Old Course, and to the left of the 9th

Longdown - the site of the holes abandoned in 1934.

hole, New Course; some remnants of them can still be seen. Apart from the 6th hole, now the 9th, the others were all abandoned in 1934.

Some years ago the author persuaded Mr. Stephen Sillem, as someone who knew and played these holes as a young man, to write an account of them:

"Although I can see the old 6th, 7th, 8th and 9th perfectly in my mind's eye, I recently tried to trace them on the ground. I was staggered to see the extent to which nature had taken over - perhaps this should not be too surprising as it must be 50 years since they were abandoned.

The old 6th was played from the present 9th tee. There were two distinct routes to the green. The long hitter could attempt to hit a long drive along the crest of the hill on the left. If he got far enough, he had a daunting shot over the side of the valley where the bridleway dips steeply down on its way to Highams Corner on the Chertsey Road. The green was cut into the hill the far side of the bridleway, and for a second shot to find the green a carry of some 180 yards was needed. The less adventurous golfer would drive down what is now the 9th fairway, play his second up to the left to a point near the bridleway from which he might hope for a clear view of the green for his third shot. An unusual and arduous hole!

The 7th tee was at the top of the hill above the 6th green. From here one drove to a fairway probably 200 feet lower than the tee. The hole was dog-leg to the right and called for a second shot of about 180 yards to a sloping green cut into the side of the hill that runs down to the corner of a fenced wood that extends down to the Chertsey Road. There is a house now just below the green.

To reach the 8th tee involved a further climb up and round this hill. The 8th was a nondescript sort of hole of about 310 yards to a green about 100 yards from the point where the fairway starts as one comes down from the 10th tee on the Old Course.

The 9th was a hole of some 375 yards - again uphill all the way - to a saddle-back green on a col leading to the top of the high hill looking down on to the 10th green and Battle's hut.

The 10th tee was at the top of this hill, and afforded a spectacular shot down on to the 10th green, which is still in play, but is approached from an entirely new direction, with the consequence that some of the bunkers now appear to be facing the wrong way.

The five holes I have attempted to describe certainly involved quite a bit of mountaineering, and would have been almost impossible for trolleys and buggies. However, in the days when caddies were plentiful, and not too highly paid, they were entertaining if not very good golf. The best of them was probably the 9th."

In 1934 an Extraordinary General Meeting was called to consider alterations to the New Course. A report by Simpson & Company, Golf Architects Ltd., had been commisioned by the Committee, and was discussed at the meeting.

Mr. Tom Simpson was a controversial, not to say eccentric character. According to Henry Longhurst he once drove his Rolls-Royce slowly up and down outside the window of a room where a club committee was deliberating whether to accept his design. He clearly had firm views on golf architecture, and two extracts from his report are worth recording:

"I am asked to say what exactly has been my intention in designing the new holes at Sunningdale as I have.

..... I have attempted - so far as the terrain at Sunningdale permitted - to introduce the spirit of St. Andrews, the world's only real golf course. Further, my intention has been to counter the mischievous results from playing with graded clubs and an altogether abominable golf ball. To that end, I have insisted that if a player goes 'all out' from the tee he must combine length with accuracy if he is to succeed. It is very certain that mere length, and a profusion of bunkers, is no answer to the problems of today. Princes Sandwich, with its 7,000 yards and many bunkers, did not stop scores under 70 in the last Championship that was played there. Princes failed for one reason, and only one; because at every hole the centre of the fairway is the best place from which to approach the green. In other words, the orientation of the green to the second shot is faulty on that course.

..... For the most part, neither golfers nor golf architects understand the true function of a fairway hazard.

..... The proper function of the first fairway hazard is to govern the play of the hole and to trap the scratch golfer's good shot, which is not quite good enough. To that end, there should be no fairway bunker within 200 yards of the tee. The first fairway bunker or hazard should be so placed that it is not more than a few yards off the scratch golfer's most favourable line to the hole. There is no necessity to bunker the wrong line to the hole if the green has been properly sited."

The E.G.M. passed Mr. Simpson's proposals unanimously. His main recommendations concerned holes 6 to 10 which were to be mostly on new ground over the back of the 5th green. This would overcome the problem of the excessive undulations of the existing holes. When Harry Colt designed these holes he was to a large extent tied to the land near the stables, as at that time all the cutting and carting was done by horses; now that the work could be done by tractor it was possible to go further afield.

Mr. Simpson made some other changes, notably to the 13th green, but his major proposals concerned new holes. In 1935, R.H. Anketell, then Captain, drove the first ball on the reconstructed course; the caddie who retrieved the ball was given a sovereign, St. Andrews fashion. However, as we shall see, the new holes were not popular, and two years later more radical changes were made. To avoid confusion, holes 6 to 10 will be dealt with together, as will the 1st and 18th holes which have also been subject to much alteration over the years, and impinge so much on one another.

1st hole, 451 yards, par 4
18th hole, 465 yards, par 5
The original tee for the 1st hole was sited between the practice chipping green and the nearby oak tree. The green was just short of the raised 2nd tee, more or less where the present 18th back tee is.

At that time the 18th tee was just below the present 1st green, with a back tee the other side of the then 1st fairway. The 18th green was just in front of where the present 1st tee is sited.

It can be seen that playing the 18th from either of its tees there was an option to go to the right or left of the pine trees dividing the two fairways. The further clump of broom and trees did not exist, and provided the drive on the left hand line was long enough, there was a clear view of the green.

However, driving this line inevitably led to some interference with players coming down the 1st. It was, therefore, decided in 1927 to reverse the 1st and 18th holes.

The 1st tee was moved to a site roughly behind the old 18th green, and the present 1st green was built. The new 18th tee was sited as now, but there have been several different sites for the 18th green. The first was as already described, the second was roughly between the two present 18th greens, another was the present practice green, and finally today's green was built after much argument in 1957 with modifications in 1967.

2nd hole, 165 yards, par 3
This hole has remained unchanged.

The approach to the 3rd green, New Course.

3rd hole, 395 yards, par 4

Modifications were made to the bunkering in 1934, and a new back tee was made in 1994, but otherwise there has been no change.

4th hole, 433 yards, par 4

As a result of the Simpson report a new green was made on the lower ground to the right of the present green. According to Stephen Sillem it was "a preposterous, tiny, hump-backed green falling away in every direction which it was quite impossible to hit from more than 20 yards." This was more than the members would stand for, and it was summarily removed when John Morrison was brought in to do some reconstruction work in 1937. The green was then restored to its former, and current, position.

Bunkers on the right and left of the fairway were taken out of use in 1966, and in 1970 a new bunker was added on the left edge of the green.

5th hole, 167 yards, par 3

The principal change to this hole concerns the tee. At first the hole was played from the present forward tee. From 1936 to 1963 it was played from the present 13th medal tee. It then reverted to the higher tee, which was extended by almost 30 yards. This involves a climb, but there is a much better view of the green.

In 1993 the two original bunkers, some thirty yards short of the green, which had to be carried to reach it, were amalgamated into a somewhat smaller one.

6th hole, 485 yards, par 5
7th hole, 365 yards, par 4
8th hole, 388 yards, par 4
9th hole, 424 yards, par 4
10th hole, 206 yards, par 3

The layout of these holes which resulted from Tom Simpson's report was quite different from the present one. Unfortunately, no map of these holes survives and the following description is the best reconstruction it has been possible to make with the aid of Simpson's report, Committee minutes, and the proposals put to the E.G.M. of 9 June, 1934.

The 6th hole was a drive and a pitch from the present forward tee to a green on the side of the hill to the left of the ponds.

Approach to 6th hole, New Course.

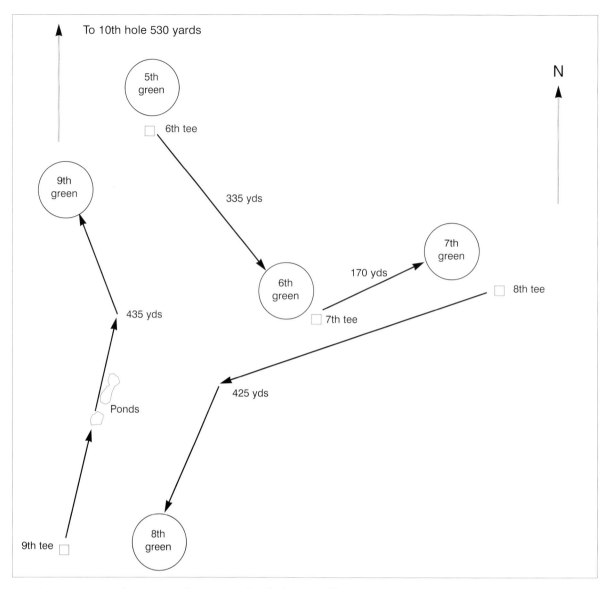

Diagrammatic layout, as far as can be deduced, of holes 6 to 9 (New Course) following Tom Simpson's report in 1934.

The player then turned left to the 7th tee for a short hole of about 170 yards to the 7th green. The trees and scrub on the top of the hill largely did not exist.

The 8th hole was played from a tee near the 7th green towards what is now the second half of the 6th fairway, thence dog-leg left to the present 6th green. A hole of 425 yards.

From a tee near the latter green the 9th tee shot was played over the swampy grounds near the ponds. The fairway must have been shared with the 6th, and was probably wider than now. The second shot was played to a green south-west of the 5th green over the ditch. The hole was approximately 440 yards.

72

10th hole, New Course.

The new 10th hole was on the line of the present 9th, but was designed as a three-shotter of 530 yards to a new green on the 11th fairway.

In 1937, J.S.F. Morrison DFC., who had been Captain of the Club in 1933, and was now a golf course architect, was asked to review the layout of these holes which evidently had encountered much criticism. Again, no record of his report, nor the action taken on it, survives, but it is fairly certain that something like the present layout resulted. In particular, the 6th hole dog-leg was created; the short 7th was scrapped, and the 8th hole was played from the present tee to a green cut into the hill behind the 5th green; the present green, further on and to the right was made in 1961. Simpson's 9th hole and 10th green were scrapped, resulting in the present 9th hole and green. The short 10th hole was revived, but from the present tee, and the 11th hole was again lengthened into the current left-hand dog-leg.

All in all, the alterations to these holes, 6 to 11 on the New, were the most radical on either course, and also the most contentious.

11th hole, 436 yards, par 4

From the account of the previous five holes it will be seen that the 11th hole is more or less now in its original form, having had a short period from a tee much further forward, making a hole of some 300 yards. It is worthy of note that the wood on the left was only a small plantation when the hole was made in the early 1920s, and there are stories of one or two occasions when the green was driven.

12th hole, 385 yards, par 4

At the time of Simpson's report in 1934 the Committee decided, in addition, to make a new 12th green to the left of the present one, on the lower ground. However, this was no more successful than Simpson's green on the 4th, and three years later the minutes record a decision "that the former New Course green be brought back into play at once."

In 1966 a long bunker on the right of the green was taken out of play and filled with heather turves.

13th hole, 543 yards, par 5

Harry Colt's original hole was over 600 yards long, and was driven from a tee above the present 5th tee to a green to the right, and 50 to 60 yards beyond the one now in use. The latter was one of Simpson's recommendations; he felt it was a much better site and shortened the hole somewhat. At the same time, bunkers on the left of the fairway, which can still be seen, were abandoned.

In 1963 the medal tee moved to the 5th tee, and the latter went back to its original, higher site.

14th hole, 181 yards, par 3

The 1934 changes involved the filling in of several bunkers on this hole. A new back tee has been built stretching the hole to its present length. Otherwise no change.

15th hole, 404 yards, par 4

This hole has given rise to some controversy from time to time. Harry Colt's layout was a right-handed dog-leg. The bank and ditch to the left of the drive ran all the way to the wood, thus splitting the fairway. The pond did not exist, but there was a ditch at right angles to the bank. Thus, the long hitter had a choice; to play the hole as a dog-leg, as intended by the

74

15th hole, New Course.

architect, or to attempt to drive the ditch on to a relatively small landing area. A slight hook and he could be in trouble; he had to think, and weigh the odds.

The filling in of part of the lateral ditch and removal of its bank gave the long hitter a large target area at which to aim, and many have questioned the wisdom of the change. The drainage of the hole was also affected. However, the development of the transverse ditch into a well-landscaped pond, and other drainage measures, have improved that aspect, and a new back tee has lengthened the carry for those trying to drive over the pond.

A bunker was added on the right front of the green in the 1960s, tightening up the second shot.

16th hole, 379 yards, par 4
This hole is virtually unchanged, apart from a new back tee made in 1993.

17th hole, 171 yards, par 3
This hole has had drainage problems, but apart from some minor bunkering changes it remains as first laid out.

The development of the 18th hole has already been described.

The Nine-Hole Course

The Nine-hole Course has now disappeared, but it has its place in the history of the Club. Just before the First World War Stephen Sillem's father built a house (Parkers Hill - now Park Hill) off the Chobham Road, and the 6th hole ran immediately behind it. Stephen started his golf on the course, and the following is his account of it.

"The 1st hole was almost identical with the present 1st hole of the New Course, although I think the green was short and left of the present green.

The tee for the 2nd hole was approximately where the 17th green of the New is, but the ground was built up to make that green. Part of the original fairway is still identifiable, running past the 17th (New) tee, passing left of the 16th green to a raised green some 100 yards further on. The green, as I recall, had heather at the back on both sides. It was all levelled off to make the approach to the 16th (New) green.

The 3rd hole was incorporated intact into the 3rd hole (New).

The 4th hole started from the 15th (New) tee nearest to the 14th green, and the drive was diagonally across the ditch and heathery bank onto the fairway which is now part of the 15th (New). The green was some 100 yards short and 60 yards left of the present green, the site now being completely in the trees. In the days of the Nine-hole Course the heathery bank and ditch I have mentioned continued right on up the hill.

The 5th was a short hole (150 yards), from a tee in front of the forward tee for the 16th (New), to a green in the elbow of the 16th fairway where it turns right towards the 16th green.

76

The 5th on the Jubilee. A general panorama of the course includes A.J. Lacey driving off from the 5th tee. As the picture shows, it's hard to believe that Sunningdale is less than an hour's journey by train from London.

The 6th was a long and splendid hole (my private practice ground) which ran from a tee at the corner of the garden of the house on the right of the 16th (New) fairway. A fine, wide, fairway with cross bunkers about 275 yards from the tee, running along the bottom of the gardens of the few houses that had then been built on Titlarks Hill to a slightly raised green which was roughly mid-way between Stearn's Farm and Parkers Hill. This entire hole has disappeared under an impenetrable jungle of trees, thorns and bushes.

The 7th hole was a hole of some 200 yards down the hill from the 6th green to a green in the angle of Titlarks Hill Road and Chobham Road. This area has now largely been built over.

To reach the 8th tee one had to cross Titlarks Hill Road to a tee about 60 yards or so from the present Club gate. I do not recall any houses on that side of Titlarks Hill Road in those days. The fairway followed the line of the road over the shoulder of the hill to a green some 300 yards distant.

The 9th was a long hole from the top of the far end of the present practice ground, across an open ditch to a green short of the Artisans' clubhouse.

The Nine-hole Course was always kept in pretty good condition. There were not many bunkers to maintain, but there was a lot of mowing involved."

The enormous increase in the amount of play on golf courses since the mid-1950s has created major greenkeeping problems, particularly on inland courses, from which Sunningdale has not been immune. When the Old Course was laid out it was common practice to build greens with the "dew-ponding" method with a clay base designed to retain rainwater. With the advent of automatic watering in 1966 the requirement was to allow the water to leach out, and in these circumstances it was easy to over-water. This, together with the heavy play compacting the surface of the greens, led to a build up of fibrous conditions underneath. Areas of meadow grass were thus encouraged to spread, and the record drought year of 1976 emphasized the seriousness of the problem.

An intensive programme of aeration was undertaken with a reduction of fertiliser treatment and irrigation. Similar action at that time was urged upon Clubs by agronomists all over the country. At Sunningdale, in addition, holes were bored in all the greens every few yards to penetrate the clay base in order to improve the drainage. In one year, from 1976 to 1977, expenditure on the courses rose from £61,000 to £92,000; by the mid-1990s it was over £600,000. Successive Committees have supported the view that the courses are the Club's principal asset and must be maintained to a high standard.

There have been less problems on the fairways. The 1976 drought led to a fairway watering system on both courses being installed in 1978, together with a reservoir in 1979, and another in 1990, giving reserves of water of 7 million gallons. Despite this, both reservoirs were dry in the 1995 drought by mid-August. Over the years, though, these reservoirs are undoubtedly saving the Club money.

By 1997 it was clear that the irrigation system in general, which was one of the first in the country, and some parts of which were 30 years old, had to a large extent reached the end of its useful life, particularly with regard to the pipe-

78

work; bursts were frequent and maintenance absorbed many man-hours. Also, the technology of golf course irrigation had made significant advances, not to increase watering, but to improve the application of water and minimise wastage.

An Irrigation Sub-Committee, under the Chairmanship of Sean Baguley, was set up and produced a thorough and detailed proposal for the installation of a completely new automatic irrigation system for both courses. The estimated cost was of the order of £600,000, and Members approved the proposal at the 1997 A.G.M.

In 1992 an extensive programme of tree and scrub clearance was started. The objective was to let in light and air to those areas, to improve the drainage of the courses, and to maintain their heathland character.

In 1998 a borehole was successfully sunk which allows the Club to draw up to eleven million gallons, raising its total water resources, including the reservoirs, to eighteen million gallons.

Greenkeeping is a continual struggle against the elements, turf diseases, pests and so on. Acknowledging this, and the problems mentioned above, the Sunningdale courses bear favourable comparison with others year in and year out, and golfers come from far and wide to play them.

DIAGRAMMATIC LAYOUT
OF THE COURSES

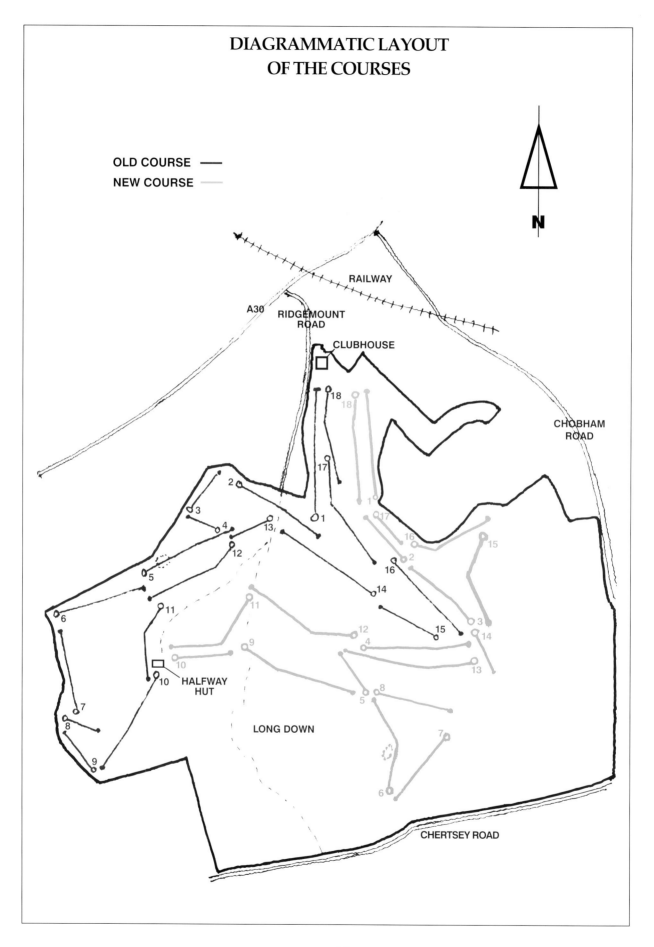

CHAPTER SIX

The Ladies

When the Old Course opened in September, 1901, the Committee decided "that for the present time Ladies be not allowed to play over the links." However, by Spring, 1902, the Annual Report stated that "the Committee have thought it advisable to allow Ladies to play, subject to certain restrictions." They were allowed to play on weekdays with the member introducing them, but not at weekends or on public holidays. They were not allowed in the clubhouse except for tea after 4.00 p.m. In 1903 the playing restrictions were relaxed to allow Ladies to play on Sundays after 3.15 p.m. in mixed foursomes. Members had to play with their lady guests and allow "ordinary two ball matches to pass" *(Appendix 5)*.

In 1907 an addition was made to the Bye-Laws: "During the months of June, July, August and September Ladies shall be allowed to play in mixed foursomes on Saturdays after 4 p.m. at a fee of three shillings".

So there was a gradual relaxation of the Bye-Laws relating to Ladies, but no further significant moves appear to have been made until after the First World War.

During the war women did splendid work in factories and elsewhere, apart from traditional occupations such as nursing. Many of the tasks they undertook had hitherto only been performed by men; as a result attitudes underwent a marked change.

The Club Committee took note of these developments, and in 1923, helped perhaps by the opening of the New Course, the following "Rules for Ladies" were drawn up:

"Mondays to Fridays
Ladies may play at any time, but only with the member or temporary member who introduces them. The green fee payable shall be 2/6d per round.

Ladies are allowed to play on only one of the courses. Information as to which course is available for them may be obtained from the Caddiemaster.

Lady members of Sunningdale Ladies Golf Club who have a L.G.U. handicap of 20 or better are granted the following privileges:

1. They need not be introduced by a member.
2. They may play together on the course allotted for the day.
3. They may introduce and play with their Lady Guests, who will pay a green fee of 2/6d.
4. They are excused a green fee.

Saturdays, Sundays, Competition Days or Public Holidays
Ladies of the S.L.G.C. have no special privileges over other Ladies, but are subject to all the general bye-laws for Ladies, i.e.:

1. They shall play only with the member or temporary member who introduces them, paying a green fee of 2/6d a round.
2. They may play only the course reserved for fourball matches.
3. They may start only at the following times: Between 11.30 a.m. and 1 p.m. After 3.15 p.m.
4. Ladies having a L.G.U. handicap of 6 or better may start at any time, provided they play with a full member.
5. Luncheons are not served to Ladies, and no Lady is allowed in the Clubhouse except for tea after 4 p.m."

The Committee also decided to make teeing grounds for Ladies on the New Course on holes 5, 7, 8 and 18. The Ladies would not be allowed to hold competitions, such as monthly medals, or matches against other Clubs, on either of the courses. Tee boxes, differing in shape from those on the men's tees, might be used, but must be white in colour without any letters painted thereon. The reason for the latter condition is not immediately apparent.

In 1924 the privilege of being excused a green fee was withdrawn from the members of the S.L.G.C., as was the right of Ladies with a L.G.U. handicap of 6 or better to play at any time as in Rule 4 above. However the time restriction in Rule 3 was reduced in the afternoon to after 3 p.m., and the restriction was not to apply to the winner and past winners of the Ladies Open Championship!

These Rules appear to have remained in force until 1950 when Associate Lady Members were admitted to the Club. However, by 1946 the rules regarding admission of Lady guests to the Clubhouse had already been relaxed. The Reading Room and Dining Room were opened to Lady Guests accompanied by members, and a member could bring two Ladies to lunch at any one time. *(Appendix 13)*

The kind of restrictions set out in the "Rules for Ladies" were commonplace at golf clubs in the 1920s, so it is of interest that Sunningdale was host to a match of international standard between American and British Lady golfers in 1930. It was the forerunner of the Curtis Cup which started in 1932. The British team won by six matches to four after what Molly Gourlay, the British Captain, described as an "intensely interesting day's golf." She won her own singles match against the American Captain Glenna Collett, by one hole.

The Club obviously put itself out for the occasion. Miss Gourlay wrote "I cannot end this account without expressing my deep gratitude and appreciation to everybody at Sunningdale who helped so nobly in making every possible arrangement for the comfort of the players."

One of the players in that match was Diana Fishwick, later Mrs. Critchley, who won the Ladies' British Open Amateur Championship in 1930, and the English Ladies' Amateur Championship in 1932 and 1949. She also won several Championships on the Continent. When the Sunningdale Foursomes started in 1934, she and her partner Noel Layton (Walton Heath) won the inaugural tournament. At that time her Club was Wentworth, but subsequently she joined Sunningdale, and for many years was Honorary Secretary and an invaluable member of the Ladies Section. She was made an Honorary Member in 1964. The mixed bar is now named the Critchley Room in tribute to her.

Her husband, Brigadier General A.C. Critchley, presented the Critchley Salver for an annual 36-hole ladies' stroke play tournament at Sunningdale; many leading lady golfers take part.

Great Britain v America. Glenna Collett's American team 1930.

Great Britain v America. Molly Gourlay's victorious team, 1930.

Golf Illustrated Gold Vase 1930. Bobby Jones being congratulated on his win by Diana Fishwick. Diana had just won the British Ladies Open Championship.

Sunningdale Foursomes winners 1934. Diana Fishwick and Noel Layton.

Another member of the Ladies Section to gain international honours is Mrs. Carole Caldwell who was twice chosen to play for the British Isles in the Curtis Cup, in 1978 and 1980.

A match in the early days of the Club which must have engendered much excitement took place in October, 1910. Miss Cecilia Leitch, then 19, an outstanding young player who was soon to start collecting her formidable total of 12 Open titles (amongst them 4 British Ladies and 2 English Ladies Championships), played a 72-hole match against Harold Hilton. He was twice a winner of the Open Championship (1892 and 1897) and of the Amateur Championship (1900 and 1901).

The first 36 holes were played at Walton Heath, and the final 36 at Sunningdale the following day. Mr. Hilton was conceding a stroke on all the even holes, and at the end of the first day was leading by one hole. After the first 18 holes at Sunningdale he went into lunch four up, and standing on the fourth tee in the afternoon he was five up - five up and fifteen to play. One account stated, "... it would hardly be too much to say .. not one single one of the spectators thought Miss Leitch had the faintest chance of avoiding defeat... nobody dreamed Mr. Hilton could lose, but he did."

He gave his opponent one or two chances, which she took, and his golf became "distinctly ragged", whereas hers started to improve, particularly her putting. Her wooden club play, on a cold, wet and windy day, had been excellent throughout the match, and by the turn she was only one down. "Mr. Hilton's lead melted away with that astonishing and paralysing rapidity which is known to every one who has ever lost a match that he ought to have won." Miss Leitch squared the match at the 10th in the teeth of the gale, won 11 and 12, lost 13 to a 2, two halves followed; she then won 16 and halved 17 to win the match by 2 up and 1 to play. She had taken approximately 77 strokes for 17 holes.

A newspaper cutting in a Club scrapbook, with a byline "Henry Leach", ends his account as follows:

"There were about a thousand people there, and the Sunningdale Club, whose course nowadays is really superb, treated them very nicely. Naturally there were more ladies than is usual in a golf crowd, and it would be a terrible thing for our eyesight if there were always so many, and the points of their hatpins stuck out so prominently. Hatpins in a golf crowd are murderous. It was a partisan crowd quite undisguised. Every time the girl made a shot of any kind they shouted "Grand shot!" and laughed and cheered. All her little ducklings were great big swans. They did not cheer Hilton. They were not intentionally unkind, but they did not really want him to win, and they overlooked his fine shots, and quite forgot about the half he was bravely giving. Probably Hilton is as little affected by this sort of thing as any man, but I know many who would not have liked it. Because of this, and because it proved nothing (what nonsense to call it a "test!"), and because somehow this mixture of excessive sentimentality did not seem quite in harmony with the idea of the strong, hard, sporting game as played by men alone, one hopes that this experiment, as a public thing, will not often be repeated, while admitting that as an occasional novelty it is excellent. Miss Leitch ought to win the ladies' championship very soon now"(She did, her first win being in 1914.)

To lady golfers in the 1930s, particularly those in the hierarchy of the Ladies Golf Union, a certain Gloria Minoprio was a revolutionary. She was the second cousin of John Minoprio, a present member of Sunningdale; this link and her place in the history of women's golf, justify an account of her appearance in the English Ladies' Championship at Westward Ho! in 1933.

Gloria, aged 26, whose real name was Dorothy, had a bye into the second round and was due on the tee in the last match of the day. Her opponent, Miss Mary Halstead, was taking some practice swings. Gloria's name was called and, just in time to avoid disqualification, a yellow Rolls-Royce drove into the car park and out she stepped. An attractive woman with a superb figure, she was immaculately dressed in a dark blue beret, matching pullover and - tightly-cut trousers! As a Swedish journalist has written, she could not have caused a bigger sensation if she had appeared stark naked!

The tweed-skirted ladies of the L.G.U. hierarchy were not amused. No lady golfer had ever before appeared on a golf links in trousers, let alone in a championship.

Nothing daunted, with an air of complete confidence she walked to the tee, acknowledged her opponent and drove off.

That was not the end of it. She had only one club! The equivalent of which today would be a one or two iron. Her caddy carried a similar club as a reserve and a supply of golf balls. From all accounts she had an excellent swing and hit the ball straight a fair distance, but she could not loft it from a hard surface or chip over a hazard.

Her opponent, despite the pressure of possibly losing to someone thus attired, playing with only one club, and not speaking a word, kept her game together and duly won by five and three.

To enter the championship a single figure L.G.U. handicap was necessary which Gloria had presumably acquired at Littlestone where she was a member. She played in the English and British Ladies' Championships until the war in 1939. She won a couple of matches, but her evident skill with just one club leaves one wondering how much better she might have been with a full set.

Henry Longhurst wrote an amusing piece about the 1933 incident entitled "Sic transit Gloria Monday". On a later occasion when Gloria beat a nervous opponent in the first round, but lost in the next, his headline was "Sic transit Gloria Tuesday". He also commented that not all that long afterwards half the field in ladies' championships turned out in trousers, "but none of them fit like Gloria Minoprio's."

As for the lady professionals in the Colgate championships at Sunningdale in their Bermuda shorts, the photographs speak for themselves.

Gloria died in 1958, but no one has ever discovered the reason for her mysterious appearances in unusual dress and playing with one club. She made a bit of golfing history, and the original trousers are said to be in the Ladies Golf Museum in London.

There have since been some remarkable lady golfers, such as Joyce Wethered, whom Sheridan said rarely took more than 72 shots off the men's tees on either course at Sunningdale, and the American, "Babe" Zaharias who won three US Ladies' Open Championships and more than 50 events during her career. However, one could say that it was not until Colgate Palmolive sponsored six Ladies' European Open Championships at Sunningdale from 1974 to 1979 that the standard reached by leading Lady Professionals, mainly American, was widely appreciated. Eyes were opened in more ways than one by the distance they hit the ball, by the excellence of their short game, by their dress, and by their demeanour. It seemed to many onlookers that they appreciated, perhaps more than their male counterparts, their principal function was to entertain their public.

Joyce Wethered winner with J.S.F. Morrison. Sunningdale Foursomes 1935 and 1936.

Mrs. Judy Rankin won the 1972 tournament (54 holes) with a total of 218, and Nancy Lopez the final 1979 tournament (72 holes) with a score of 282. Colgate Palmolive then withdrew its sponsorship, and a tournament which all who came to watch had enjoyed, sadly ended.

In 1997 the Club was host to the Weetabix Women's British Open Championship on the Old Course. The international field included top women players from the American and European professional Tours as well as from the Japanese Tour.

The Championship was blessed with fine weather except for the last hours of the final round when there was a heavy downpour. Large crowds followed the play and, as with the Colgate Championships twenty years earlier, the spectators were much impressed with the quality of the golf and the distance the players hit the ball. 26 players were on par 288 or better after the final round.

The winner was the young Australian Karrie Webb, who had previously won in 1995 in her first full year as a professional. Her winning score was 269, 8 shots clear of the runner-up Rosie Jones (USA), which included a remarkable third round of 63.

Helen Alfredsson, winner of the Championship in 1990, also scored a 63 in the pro-am.

There was some disappointment that several well-known players such as Nancy Lopez, Pat Bradley and Marie-Laure de Lorenzi, failed to qualify for the final two rounds. Laura Davies gave her supporters much enjoyment with some prodigious hitting, but they had hoped for a better total than 287.

Players, Championship officials and spectators much praised the Club for their reception and the condition of the course.

The impression created by these Lady Professionals will endure, and although in the nature of things they would never be favourites in a head-to-head match with the top men professionals, club players can probably learn more from watching them swing the club than they can from the "gorillas" of the men's circuit.

The lady golfers in 1903 who could only play at the Club as guests in mixed Foursomes on Sunday afternoon would doubtless be astonished at the rights and privileges of today's Associate Lady Members. In the five decades since they were admitted to the Club, their section has grown to over 70 Full and Junior Members with almost as many again in various other categories of membership, such as Country, Overseas, and Five-Day. There are over fifty stroke and match-play events during the year, and there is no restriction on playing rights, although most play during the week, leaving the weekend mainly to the men. Their subscriptions are at a significant discount to those of men members.

It can confidently be said that the foresight and expectations of the members who voted in 1950 to admit Lady Associates have been fully justified.

CHAPTER SEVEN

Golf and the Golfers at Sunningdale

In the hundred years of the Club's existence there have been many more than that number of important professional and amateur tournaments and events held over its courses. Club members have won national and international honours, not necessarily at the time of their membership, and some of its professionals have been among the leading players of their day. What follows records the achievements of many of these notable players, and describes certain events which have taken place at the Club.

Challenge Match - Jack White v. Tom Vardon

In the closing years of the last century and the early years of this one, professionals often played challenge money matches. In November, 1902, when the course had been open barely a year, Sunningdale was the venue for the second half of a 72-hole home-and-away match for £50 a side between Jack White, the Club professional, and Tom Vardon of Sandwich.

The opening hole of the Sandwich match was described by John Low of Cambridge University in a newspaper article. Approaching the first green from long grass off his second shot Vardon had a 'dunch', which nevertheless left his ball six feet from the hole. Mr. Low helpfully explained that a 'dunch' is a "digging downward class of stroke." White, who had bunkered his second, came out too strongly and, although just on the green, lay a long way from the pin. After Vardon had missed his putt for a four, White holed a difficult second putt for a hard-won half.

White won the second hole and Vardon the seventh, and the match was all square at the turn. With Vardon winning three holes, and White two, on the back nine Vardon was one up after 18 holes. The fourteenth was a two-hole swing. It was won by Vardon after hitting his second shot out of bounds on the right, but reaching the green in four and holing a long putt for five. White, who was just short in two, took four more to get down and lost a hole he should have won. The scores were Vardon 76, White 78.

In the afternoon they reached the turn all square, White having won three holes to Vardon's two, but again on the back nine Vardon won three holes to White's two, so at the end of the first 36 holes Vardon was still leading by one hole; the scores being White 74, Vardon 75.

Writing about the Sunningdale half of the match Mr. Low commented, "If the Haskell is to be the standard then Sunningdale must be considered as standing almost alone in England as a test of golf. With a gutta ball the ordinary driver finds the holes too long, the round too weary a work to encourage repetition. The new factor which has killed the old courses has given life to this Sunningdale green and made it attractive instead of dull."

Mr. Low was severely critical of the short holes at Sunningdale - the 4th, 8th and 13th, as all having blind tee shots. None of these holes was popular with members, and as mentioned elsewhere, all were altered subsequently.

In the morning at Sunningdale White was round in 74 - a record - which enabled him to start the final 18 holes two up. After lunch he won the first two holes with birdies to go four up. When three halves followed he was four up and thirteen to play, and seemed on his way to winning. However, he was in trouble at the sixth, having hooked his tee shot, and lost the hole. He also lost the ninth, but won the eleventh to restore his lead to three up with seven to play. Vardon then won the 12th, 14th and 15th to go all square. With his lead gone and the holes slipping away White lost the 16th and 17th to lose the match and the money. There was excellent play from both players, in particular White's 74s at Sandwich and Sunningdale, but Vardon was the stronger man and this told in the end.

"News of the World" Match Play Championship, 1903

This was the first of five occasions that this Championship was played at the Club, the last being in 1922.

"NEWS OF THE WORLD" MATCH PLAY TOURNAMENT,

to be played at SUNNINGDALE, by the kind permission of the Sunningdale Golf Club, on

TUESDAY, WEDNESDAY & THURSDAY, 13th, 14th & 15th OCTOBER, 1903.

First Prize, £100 ; Second Prize, £30 ; Third & Fourth Prizes, £15 each : Fifth, Sixth, Seventh & Eighth Prizes, £10 each.

THE DRAW.

FIRST ROUND. 13th October (Morning).	SECOND ROUND. TUESDAY, 13th October (Afternoon).	THIRD ROUND. WEDNESDAY, 14th October (Morning).	SEMI-FINAL. WEDNESDAY, 14th October (Afternoon).	FINAL (36 Holes). THURSDAY, 15th October. Starting at 10.30 & 2.30.
Player and Club. ARTHUR GRAY, Gravesend / W. MACNAMARA, Lahinch	ARTHUR GRAY ... 3 & 1			
T. SIMPSON, Timperley / J. H. TAYLOR, Mid-Surrey	J. H. TAYLOR ... 3 & 1	J. H. TAYLOR ... 2 & 1		
J. MILNE, Neasden / A. H. SCOTT, Elie	A. H. SCOTT ... 3 & 2	ALEX. HERD ... 4 & 3	J. H. Taylor 3+1	
ALEX. HERD, Huddersfield / G. CARTER, unattached	ALEX. HERD ... 7 & 6			James Braid 4+2
W. TOOGOOD, Ilkley / JAMES HEPBURN, Home Park	JAMES HEPBURN ... 2 up			
JACK ROSS, Sutton / JAMES BRAID, Romford	JAMES BRAID ... 6 & 5	JAMES BRAID ... 5 & 4	James Braid at 19th ho	
H. CAWSEY, Ashford Manor / A. H. TOOGOOD, Headingley	A. H. TOOGOOD ... 5 & 3	A. A. TOOGOOD ... 1 up		
JACK WHITE, Sunningdale / TOM WILLIAMSON, Notts	TOM WILLIAMSON ... 1 up			
J. OLUCAS, Bamford / J. FORRESTER, Earlsferry	J. FORRESTER ... 2 & 1	J. FORRESTER ... 2 & 1		
R. THOMSON, North Berwick / G. RALPH SMITH, West M dsl sx	R. THOMSON ... 4 & 3	J. G. COBURN ... 4 & 3	J. G. Coburn 5+4	E. Ray 4+3
W. T. JEFFRIES, Hallowes / J. G. COBURN, Portmarnock	J. G. COBURN ... 3 & 2			
J. SHERLOCK, Oxford / WILLIE FERNIE, Troon	WILLIE FERNIE ... On 19th			
EDWARD RAY, Ganton / JOHN ROWE, Ryl. Ashdown Forest	EDWARD RAY ... 3 & 2			
TOM VARDON, Ryl. St. George's / P. WYNNE, Tooting Bec	TOM VARDON ... 3 & 2	EDWARD RAY ... 7 & 6	E. Ray 2+1	
J. W. WHITING, Walmley / ROWLAND JONES, Wimbld'n Pk.	ROWLAND JONES ... 6 & 4	ROWLAND JONES ... 7 & 5		
A. MITCHELL, St L'nards-on-Sea / DAVID HERD, Littlestone-on-Sea	DAVID HERD ... 1 up			

James Braid 4+3

Draw for 1903 News of the World Match Play Championship

News of the World Match-Play Championship 1903. Braid driving.

The Championship took place on the 13th, 14th and 15th October, 1903, and 32 professionals competed. Among them were J.H. Taylor, Alex Herd, James Braid, Jack White, J. Sherlock, Ted Ray and Tom Vardon. Braid won, beating Ted Ray 4 and 3 in the final over 36 holes.

10th hole: News of the World Match-Play Championship 1903.

Club Autumn Meeting: 23 and 24 October, 1903

A record of this meeting survives in a cutting from "Golf" magazine in its November, 1903, edition. The scores of all the competitors are recorded, together with the following comment:

"The Sunningdale meeting was held on October 23 and 24. The course, owing to the extraordinary rainfall, was on the heavy side, but at the same time reflected great credit on the greenkeeper, Hugh McLean. Considerable progress has been made during the past twelve months, and the wet summer has proved of great assistance. There were fortunately two fine days for the meeting, and although the wind on the first day was somewhat troublesome, the conditions otherwise were good.

Mr. Denys Scott won the Club Gold Medal with a good score of 82, his brother taking 86 being rather unfortunate in finding an unplayable lie in the heather at the fifth hole for which he took 8. The handicap prize on the second day fell to Mr. P.C. Millard with an extremely good net return of 77 (84-7)."

P.C. Millard was the father of "Bunny" Millard, a scratch player, and a stalwart of the Halford Hewitt Tournament; "Bunny" was in the Lancing team for many years.

Such accounts of Club events in golf magazines and national newspapers ceased long ago.

Challenge Match, 14 May 1904 Jack White v. Ted Ray

Sir George Newnes put up a purse for this match at Sunningdale. Ted Ray was attached to the Scarborough Club.

A strong wind was blowing, and although Ray was outdriving White, his short game in the morning round was not equal to White's. Nevertheless, having been two down with six to play he squared the match on the sixteenth, halved the seventeenth, and with a four at the long eighteenth ended the round one up. They both took about 81.

After lunch Ray increased his lead to three up after five holes. White reduced this to one playing the fourteenth, but standing on the seventeenth tee Ray was dormy. White won the seventeenth, and on the eighteenth green was left with a putt of some 15 feet to win the hole, which he duly sank to halve the match. He was round in 79, and Ray was again approximately 81.

Golf Illustrated, in reporting the match, commented that the course was in splendid order, and that a large crowd followed the play.

Jack White - Open Champion 1904

Not many Clubs are favoured with an Open Champion as their professional, and since the advent of the tournament circuit in the latter half of this century, it is unlikely that any Club will again have that honour. The day of the Club professional winning the Open has long gone.

However, when Jack White won the Open at Sandwich in 1904 Sunningdale joined a select band, and the history of the Club deserves an account of the Championship. The following is based on a report in Golf Illustrated.

In 1899, aged 26, when the Open was also played at Sandwich, White had a score of 315 as runner-up to Harry Vardon who won with 310. In the four years since then he had been three times in the top ten, being third in 1903, so his victory was no great surprise, but he was chased all the way by J.H. Taylor, James Braid, the Vardon brothers, J. Sherlock and A. Kirkaldy. In the end he won by the slimmest margin of one stroke.

On the first day there was a very strong wind which made putting exceedingly difficult. Harry Vardon, the holder, came in with a 76 having driven well, but did not putt with his usual skill. White had a round of 80, but it has to be said that in a field of 144 competitors only 9 were less than that figure.

The second day saw some lower scoring, with Harry Vardon leading the field with 73 and a total of 149. White had a 75 for 155, but the sensation of the day was J. Sherlock, the Oxford University professional, who returned a 71, including eight threes. His figures were: OUT: 4, 6, 3, 4, 4, 3, 5, 3, 3 = 35; IN: 5, 4, 3, 6, 5, 4, 3, 3, 3 = 36 - Total: 71. This left him with 154 in fourth place.

46 professionals and 6 amateurs on 168 or better qualified for the final two rounds.

On the third day the weather was ideal for golf, some light showers in the morning slowing the greens, and a warm, sunny afternoon. Harry Vardon was out early on and took most of the crowd with him. He did not play well by his standards, having five fives and a six for 79. Braid, however, was burning up the course being out in 31, and finishing the second nine with four successive threes. He set a new course record of 69, and due to this excellent play was the leader by one stroke from White who also had a good score of 72. For the final round there were four players within three strokes of the leader, White, Taylor and the two Vardons.

White was out first of this group and covered the first six holes in twenty strokes; he was out in 32. He played steadily in, and on the occasions he was in the rough made splendid recoveries, including one at the 18th hole where he pulled his drive into long grass but still got down in four for a 69 and a Championship total of 296. This was four less than Harry

Vardon's winning score the previous year, and it looked as though White was going to win.

However, all was not over as Braid stood on the 16th tee needing 3, 4, 4 to tie with White. He failed to get his three at the 16th, so ended with 71 for 297.

There was more excitement to come, as J.H. Taylor had gone out in 31 and had started back 4, 4, 3. He came to the 18th needing a three to tie with White. He did not get it, but still ended with yet another course record of 68 for a total of 297, equal with Braid, but one behind White.

So Jack White became champion, winning the championship cup, a gold medal and £50.

Jack White, the Open Champion.

His rounds were:

First Round	4	4	4	7	4	4	6	3	5	=	41	
	4	4	4	5	5	4	5	4	4	=	39	- 80
Second Round	5	5	3	4	4	3	5	3	5	=	37	
	4	4	5	5	5	5	3	3	4	=	38	- 75
Third Round	5	3	3	5	4	3	4	3	4	=	34	
	5	4	3	5	4	5	3	4	5	=	38	- 72
Fourth Round	4	4	3	4	2	3	5	3	4	=	32	
	4	4	4	5	4	4	4	4	4	=	37	- 69

Harry and Tom Vardon v. Jack White and James Braid

This was a foursome match in October, 1904, over 36 holes at Sunningdale with a purse of forty sovereigns put up by the Club.

After an early exchange of holes halves followed, and the match was square playing the eighth where White, with a putt for a win, was too strong and left his partner a stymie. Braid not only failed to negotiate the stymie but knocked the Vardons' ball in and lost the hole. At the end of the round the Vardons were one up, and both sides took 79.

In the afternoon several holes were exchanged in the first nine, but the Vardons remained one up at the turn. White and Braid won the eleventh to square the match, but the Vardons went ahead again winning the fourteenth. The fifteenth was halved, but the Vardons won sixteen and seventeen to win the match three and one. They had gone round in about 78 to their opponents 81.

When the Captain of Sunningdale, Mr. H.C. Clarke, presented the prizes of £25 to the winners and £15 to the losers he also announced that members of the Club had raised a sum of some £70 for White in recognition of his win in the Open Championship. White thanked the members for their generosity and praised the condition of the course, practice on which had enabled him to play the game he did at Sandwich.

Arthur Lees

Arthur was a fine professional golfer and a "character"; to write about him is a task one faces with some trepidation, as his memory is still fresh in the minds of many members and others who will all have their own recollections of him.

Arthur was born in Sheffield on 21 February, 1908, and died in Windsor on 26 March, 1992. As a boy aged nine he was fascinated by golf and became a caddie; by 1923 he was assistant professional at Lees Hall, Sheffield, where his game rapidly matured in between cleaning members' clubs and shoes. Around 1930 he became professional at Marienbad in Czechoslovakia where he started to become involved in profitable money matches. After several years there he returned home and took up an appointment as professional at Dore and Totley, Sheffield. His younger brother, Walter, was assistant professional and clubmaker there.

In 1939 Arthur won the Irish Open Championship. Then came the war and service in the police in Sheffield.

In 1947 he was a late choice for the Ryder Cup team, and this enabled him to qualify for the Dunlop Masters Tournament at Little Aston. His four round total was 283, which tied for first place with the Australian, Norman von Nida. There was a 36-hole play-off, and at the end of the first round Arthur was leading by five strokes. After lunch von Nida had a 69, but Arthur gave nothing away and with a round of 70 was the winner by four strokes. As Tom Scott in Golf Illustrated remarked, it was ironic that but for the Ryder Cup place Arthur would not have been playing in the tournament at all; and that certainly it proved his selection was thoroughly justified. He also said that Arthur's victory was an extremely popular one, "for there are few finer golfers in the country, and there is no one more modest or unassuming." Not everyone would agree with the latter assessment!

The 1947 Ryder Cup at Portland, Oregon, was a disaster for the British team which lost by 11 matches to one. Arthur played in the top foursome with Henry Cotton against "Porky" Oliver and Lew Worsham and lost ten and nine. Arthur also lost his single by two and one to Byron Nelson.

In 1948 and 1949 Arthur won the Midland Professional Championship, and in June, 1949, began his long association with Sunningdale when he accepted the post of professional after the death of Percy Boomer.

In the 1949 Ryder Cup at Ganton he played with Dick Burton in the foursomes and beat Sam Snead and Lloyd Mangrum by one hole, but he lost his single against Jimmy Demaret by seven and six.

Arthur Lees. Professional 1949-1976.
Honorary Member 1956.

1951 at Pinehurst, North Carolina, was Arthur's best Ryder Cup result. Although the British team were trounced by two matches to nine with one halved, Arthur played an heroic part, and took his revenge on Porky Oliver. In the foursomes with Charlie Ward he beat Porky and Henry Ransom by two and one, and in his single again beat Porky, also by two and one. In the morning round of the foursome Arthur and his partner played the last five holes in 3 2 5 3 3, which not surprisingly took them into lunch three up. In the afternoon

Arthur Lees playing from a bunker in his match against Ed Oliver. Pinehurst, 1951 Ryder Cup.

they played steadily, if not so spectacularly, to win on the penultimate green. In his single Arthur established an early lead, and despite not having a particularly good day on the greens, held on to win also on the 35th green. He was the only singles winner, and his foursome was the only one to gain a point. On his return home the Club held a cocktail party in his honour, and made a presentation.

Arthur won the Penfold Tournament in 1951, and again in 1953 which was the year of the next Ryder Cup. However, he was not selected for the team, which was rather remarkable in view of his excellent performance in the previous match, and the fact that the venue was Wentworth which he knew like the back of his hand. The team was selected by the P.G.A. Tournament Committee after a series of trial matches at Wentworth; Henry Cotton was the captain, and no doubt had a major influence on the selection. Arthur gave the impression that whilst conceding Henry Cotton's ability ("good player, mind you", he would say) they did not get on. Perhaps the ten and nine defeat in 1947 was a factor in their relationship.

Arthur was back in the team in 1955 in Palm Springs, losing his foursome, but winning his single against Marty Furgol by three and one.

Towards the end of his tournament career he won the Southern England Professional Championship in 1956, the Wentworth Foursomes in 1957, and the British Seniors Championship in 1959.

Arthur was always ready for a gamble, on or off the course. On one occasion he gave a four up start in a level match with Major Dalt Henderson (+2), and backed himself against anyone who wished to back the Major. Most of the money was on the Major, who was out in 34, but Arthur took only 27 strokes and was three up. He won the match comfortably, and a considerable sum of money.

David Foster, Bob Dimpfl and Dalt Henderson.

In the clubhouse Arthur, with his Yorkshire accent undiminished, was a great raconteur, and in his shop was a good salesman.

"I can't seem to get on with this putter."

"Let's have a look at it. You'll never putt with that, mister, shaft's bent."

One of his classic sales took place shortly before he retired, and was trying to dispose of his stock. Gordon Wolsey, a member for many years, was suffering from the unusual, but not unknown, complaint of getting "stuck at the top". So he booked a lesson with Arthur who began as usual, "Let's see you swing; and again. There's only one thing that'll cure you, mister, I say, and that's a new set of clubs. You can't play golf with clubs like those." So off they went to the shop, and Gordon did buy a new set of clubs, and it did cure him!

Lessons with Arthur were valued by the top pros, and for amateurs of no great ability it was worth a guinea a minute. With them it would go something like this. "Open your stance a bit, ball further forward. Now complete your backswing, and go through the ball." The ball is hit. "That's better, Arthur." "Better! I tell you, mister, I wish I could hit 'em like that!"

On the first tee, after lengthy negotiations about strokes and stakes, "Arthur, are we playing winter rules? " "No, we're playing golf!"

At the age of 63 Arthur was in constant pain and was losing a lot of weight. He was diagnosed as having cancer and had a major operation. Recovering in hospital the padre looked in to see him, and was greeted with, "I'm not ready for you yet!" When he returned home he was under eight stone, and those who went to see him were sure he would not survive, but he did. Only a short time afterwards he started to play golf again and had another 27 on the front nine of the Old Course (333 334 323). Truly amazing. He continued to play good golf for some years, and on 21 February, 1983, over 80 of his friends gave him a dinner at the Club on his 75th birthday.

75th Birthday. Arthur Lees and the Captain Maj. Gen. Peter Leuchars.

The Presentation.

John Whitfield (Captain 1971) and Michael Williams (Daily Telegraph).

Peter Alliss proposed the toast Chappie Snowden (Captain 1957) and Nicholas Royds (Captain 1973).

His indomitable spirit carried him through recurrences of his cancer, but in 1989 at the age of 81 he finally gave up his golf. He continued to visit the Club and give young and old the benefit of his golfing experience until quite shortly before he died in 1992.

In 1956 Arthur was made an Honorary Member of the Club. In 1973, on the occasion of his 65th birthday, he gave the Club a beautiful oak table, and in 1984 he gave his Dunlop Masters Salver for an annual scratch and handicap event, and his Irish Medal for a mixed tournament. With these gifts, and his portrait hanging in the Clubhouse, his memory will long be preserved.

The Amateur Championship and Sunningdale

Over the years quite a few Sunningdale members have been involved in the final stages of this Championship. In 1905 The Hon. Osmund Scott was runner-up at Prestwick. In 1906 at Hoylake three members were in the semi-final; Harry Colt, then Secretary, E.R. Smirke and C.C. Lingen. Colt lost to James Robb, who then beat Lingen four and three, so the Club was denied a victory.

In 1920 Cyril Tolley won the Championship at Muirfield beating Robert Gardner (USA) at the 37th hole.

In 1924 Eustace Storey, who had been Captain of the Cambridge University golf team the previous year, reached the final against Ernest Holderness. Storey was described by Harold Hilton as a much better golfer than one was apt to judge him, and one who had a habit of winning matches against the strongest of opponents.

The venue was St. Andrews and Holderness, then one of the best amateur golfers in the country, was the favourite to win. Storey, however, started strongly and it looked as though he would end the morning round three up. He had been putting well, but missed a short one on the sixteenth and again at the last, so instead of lunching three up his lead was down to one.

In the afternoon he was two down at one point, his putting touch having deserted him. Nevertheless, he had squared the match by the twelfth tee. Thereafter his putting continued to let him down, and he lost by three and two.

However, Storey went on to play in three Walker Cup matches, and in 1938 was the leading amateur in the Open Championship.

In 1929 Cyril Tolley won the title for the second time, beating John Smith, a carpenter from Elie in Fife, by four and three at Sandwich. According to Golf Illustrated Smith was a good, completely orthodox, golfer of no mean merit. In the semi-final he had beaten John Dawson (USA) on the 19th hole after being three down with three to play. A British winner of the Cup was thus assured.

Cyril Tolley - Amateur Champion 1929.

The morning round of the final ended all square. After lunch Tolley was five up after eight holes, but Smith came back at him and won the next three holes. Tolley then holed a good putt for a half at the 12th, won the 13th and had an excellent four at the 14th - 520 yards in the eye of the wind - and became dormy four. On the 15th green Tolley lay four feet from the pin with two for the Championship.

He missed the putt, but laid his opponent a dead stymie. Smith putted - for nothing - hit Tolley's ball and stayed out, so the score went down as a gentlemen's four and three, and Cyril Tolley had won the Championship for the second time.

In 1931 John de Forest (later Count John de Bendern) lost in the final by one hole to E. Smith at Westward Ho. The following year he won the Championship at Muirfield beating E. Fiddian by three and one.

In 1933 T. (Dale) Bourn lost in the final to the Hon. M. Scott at Hoylake by four and three.

In 1937 Robert Sweeney Jr. (USA) won the title beating L. Munn by three and two at Sandwich.

Robert Sweeney Jnr. - Amateur Champion 1937.

After the last war, in 1946, Gerald Micklem reached the semi-final at Birkdale. He lost to Robert Sweeney Jr., who was runner-up in the final to James Bruen.

In 1949 S.M. (Max) McCready gave British golf a great boost by first defeating the reigning champion, Frank Stranahan (USA), and then Willie Turnesa (USA) in the final by two and one, so bringing the Cup back across the Atlantic.

The Championship was played at Portmarnock, and in the morning round of the final McCready had a superb score of 70 and lunched four up; but for some fine recovery shots by Turnesa he would have been even more ahead.

In the afternoon a violent thunderstorm broke out, and by the end of the first nine holes Turnesa had squared the match. At the eleventh he went one up, but by the sixteenth they were square again. All square and three to play. McCready then won a hole he could well have lost, and with a four at the seventeenth won the match.

According to Golf Illustrated, the scene at the end was memorable. McCready was submerged by a deluge of Irish delirious with delight. Men and women danced jigs, man embraced man unashamedly. The Cup was back, and it had come to Ireland. All over Ireland the toast was the new champion, Max McCready.

Max McCready - Amateur Champion 1949.

In 1965 Clive Clark was runner-up in the Championship before turning professional, and in 1970 Bruce Critchley reached the semi-final.

In 1976 John Davies lost to Dick Siderowf (USA) in the final at the 37th hole. It was the second time Siderowf had won the Cup. Davies had beaten him in the Walker Cup match at Brookline in 1973, and this time was on home ground at St. Andrews. The omens were good for a British win, but in a long, tough, final both players had their share of mistakes on the huge St. Andrews greens. They finished the 36 holes all square, and on the 37th Davies three-putted to lose the match.

Finally, mention must be made of two of our Honorary Members. Joe Carr, who won the Championship three times, and Michael Bonallack who won it five times.

There, for the moment, rests Sunningdale's connection with the later stages of the Amateur Championship.

The Walker Cup and Sunningdale

Through the years many members of British Walker Cup teams have been associated with Sunningdale.

In the first match in America in 1922 Cyril Tolley partnered Bernard Darwin in the top foursome and lost by eight and seven to J.P. Guilford and Francis Ouimet. Guilford also beat Tolley two and one in the top single. However, at St. Andrews in 1923 Tolley had his revenge, winning both his foursome and his single. He was also a member of the team in 1924, 1926, 1930 and 1934. In his six matches he lost four foursomes and won two; similarly, he lost four singles, one of them in 1926 to Bobby Jones by twelve and eleven, and won two. Jones was then at the height of his powers, and in the 1928 match beat T.P. Perkins by thirteen and eleven!

Other players in the 1920s were Eustace Storey and Denis Kyle, who later became Captain of Sunningdale in 1936.

In the 1930s, the Hartley brothers played, (Rex in 1930 and 1932 and Lister in 1932) but sadly failed to win a point between them. John de Forest (1932) suffered the same fate. Leonard Crawley (1932, 1934, 1938 and 1947) won both the foursomes he played, lost three singles and won one.

The 1934 match was won by the United States by nine matches to two and one halved. Cyril Tolley and Harry Bentley were Sunningdale members in the team, but neither gained a point. An article in Golf Illustrated was severely critical of the method of team selection, of the captain also playing in the match, and the lack of intensive practice. The Americans, the author said, do not play any single shot better than our players. They simply play the good ones more often, and that is due to their appreciation of the essential importance of practice.

He also ridiculed the "horses for courses" method of selection - "an unreliable player is an unreliable player anywhere and everywhere"; the argument that certain courses would be too difficult for the Americans - "a good player is the master of any course or links"; and finally, "let us have no more of this praying for wind and rain and cold in the hope that the Americans cannot overcome such difficulties. Since 1921, Hutchison, Hagen, Barnes, Jones, Armour, Sarazen, Wood and Shute have been proving the utter stupidity of such prayers."

Whether as a result of such criticism or not, the next match in 1936 had six new players and a non-playing captain, but they lost by nine matches to nil with three halved. This was John Langley's first match, but he gained no points; Harry Bentley halved his single and lost his foursome.

In 1938 Great Britain and Ireland at last won a match by seven matches to four with one halved. Leonard Crawley was back in the team, winning his foursome, but losing his singles. Harry Bentley lost his foursome, and did not play in the singles.

After the Second World War the pattern of American dominance resumed, and they won another nine matches before Clive Clark at Baltimore in 1965 holed his long putt on the last hole of the crucial match to halve it and bring the overall score to eleven matches each with one halved. However, it has to be said that before the final round of eight singles Great Britain and Ireland led by ten matches to five with one halved, so the Americans once again dashed the cup of victory from our lips.

Leonard Crawley and 'Laddie' Lucas played together at St. Andrews in the 1947 foursomes and won the match, but neither won his single.

Max McCready and Gerald Micklem played in the 1949 match at Winged Foot, but neither gained a point.

After the match Dr. John Williams, President of the Oak Hill Club at Rochester N.Y. arranged for a fine Pin Oak to be dedicated in commemoration of the British team's visit for the 1949 U.S. Amateur Championship. He later sent some acorns from the tree to Wing Commander P.B. Lucas, the Captain, for distribution to the team members. Gerald Micklem planted his at the Wildernesse, and Max McCready's was put by the 14th tee of the Old Course at Sunningdale.

Leonard Crawley

In 1951 John Langley, Max McCready, and Ian Caldwell played at Birkdale. Langley halved his foursome, but lost his single. McCready did not play in the foursomes, and lost his single. Caldwell lost his foursome by one hole, but halved his single. His singles match caused much excitement. His opponent, H.D. Paddock Jr., got off to a great start and was five up after seven holes. The Golf Illustrated report stated " ... (Caldwell) stuck to his guns, and with the American failing to keep up his display, Caldwell full of fight and good golf, performed a miracle and set the last green crowd almost delirious by finishing with a one-hole lead. It was a transformation with a vengeance."

In the afternoon he forged ahead until he was three up and four to play. Then partly because he had to wait to play every shot due to the crowd his concentration relaxed a little, and after Paddock's ball had been stopped by the crowd at the 17th, and he had hooked his second at the last, he had in the end to be content with a halved game.

Gerald Micklem and John Langley played in 1953 at Kittansett, Mass., Gerald winning their only point in his foursome.

In 1955 Micklem, Caldwell and Philip Scrutton were the Sunningdale players at St. Andrews, the only winner being Caldwell beating D. Morey by one hole in his single. On the last green Ian gave his supporters a fright by missing from four feet, but "the situation was saved by his opponent unbelievably missing from a shorter distance."

Tom Scott, writing in Golf Illustrated, was critical of the fact that neither Blair nor Caldwell, the only British winners, were selected for the previous, 1953, match.

Ian Caldwell
- Walker Cup match 1955.

Sunningdale players in the 1957 match at Minikahda were Philip Scrutton and Guy Wolstenholme. Scrutton gained no points, but Wolstenholme halved his foursome and won his single. Gerald Micklem was the non-playing captain, as he was

114

for the next match in 1959 at Muirfield, Guy Wolstenholme then being the sole Sunningdale player. He lost both his foursome and his single.

David Frame played in 1961 at Seattle, but without success.

The 1963 match saw the start of the two-day matches; two rounds of foursomes, and two of singles, with a total of 24 points at stake, but there was no Sunningdale representative.

Michael King and Bruce Critchley played at Milwaukee in 1969. Michael came away with no points, but Bruce halved one foursome and won the other, and lost one single and halved the other. The second day's games were played in sweltering heat, and the British team played extremely well to win five points - three wins and four halves. The Americans won the match ten - eight with six halved.

The promising form shown in 1969 turned into victory at St. Andrews in 1971 by twelve matches to ten with two halved. R.J. (Roddy) Carr, second son of Joe Carr, played a major part, winning three and a half points out of four.

John Davies and Michael King played at Brookline (USA) in 1973, John winning both his singles, halving one foursome and losing the other. Michael halved his foursome and won his single on the first day, but lost both matches on the second day. The Cup was won by the Americans twelve - eight with four halved.

Michael turned professional in 1974, and played in the 1979 Ryder Cup.

In 1975 at St. Andrews John Davies lost both foursomes, but halved one single and won the other.

In 1977 at Shinnecock Hills he gained no points. He played finally in 1979 at Muirfield, only in the first day's singles when he lost to D. Clark. At the time of writing John is the last Sunningdale member to have played in the Walker Cup.

One cannot conclude an account of Sunningdale's involvement with the Cup without mentioning two matters.

First, the record of our two Honorary Members, Joe Carr and Michael Bonallack. Joe played in ten matches - 1947 to 1963 and 1967 (captain), and Michael in nine matches from 1957 to 1973 inclusive (captain in 1971 and 1973).

In 1987 the Cup was played at Sunningdale over the Old Course on 27th and 28th May. The Club was approached in December, 1983, by the Royal and Ancient with an invitation to stage the Walker Cup in 1987. Needless to say, the Captain at that time, Graham Young, replied that the Club was honoured to be chosen as the venue, and would do everything possible to ensure it was a successful event.

It was indeed a unique invitation as it was the first time the matches would be played on an inland course. Traditionally, the matches, and the Amateur and Open Championships, had been held on seaside links. So it was a great challenge for the Club to present the course and the clubhouse to the high standard for which it was renowned.

A Walker Cup Committee was set up as follows:

Gerald Micklem C.B.E.	President
John Mathew Q.C.	Captain
Nicholas Royds	Chairman
Derek Davies	Deputy Chairman
Jeffrey Agate	
Mrs. Patsy Boardman	
Ted Harker	
John Tullis	
Richard Thompson	Vice Captain
Keith Almond	Secretary

The following were co-opted members of the Committee: John Boardman, David Davies, Cecil Elliott, The Hon. Rocco Forte, Michael Hughesdon, Mervyn Jones, Chris Knocker, James Puckridge, Mrs. Anita Thomas (Lady Captain).

Meetings took place with Michael Bonallack, Secretary of the R.&A., and members of the R.&A. Championship Committee, and in 1985 some of the Sunningdale Walker Cup Committee joined R.&A. officials at Pine Valley Golf Club for the 1985 matches. A visit which proved extremely helpful for the Club's planning, and during which the party were made most welcome by the Pine Valley members.

Although the matches last only two days, the background administration and planning for such an event is formidable. Crowd control, car parking, tented village, leader boards, scorers, caddies, catering and so on were all allotted to the various members of the Club's Cup Committee.

A comprehensive entertainment programme was drawn up for the teams, U.S.G.A. and R.&A. officials and their wives. Members of the Club held dinner parties for the guests, and on one evening Nicholas Royds and John Mathew held a party at Nicholas's home for all the officials, wives, and other overseas dignitaries, as well as Club members acting as hosts or helpers.

Mrs. Patsy Boardman did sterling work organising visits and entertainment for wives of the teams and officials. A splendid brochure in colour was produced, co-ordinated by John Boardman and Jeffrey Agate. Ted Harker arranged golf at nearby courses for U.S.G.A. and R.&A. officials. Mrs. Anita Thomas, the Lady Captain, was in charge of the Information Centre. John Tullis, with wide experience from previous major events, organised the stewarding and crowd control arrangements. Manpower was provided by Sunningdale Artisans and volunteers from neighbouring clubs. A band of the Royal Marines played at the Flag Raising ceremony, and the event was televised by the B.B.C.

Altogether it was a magnificent team effort. The match result was disappointing, and there was some criticism of the ommision of P. McEvoy and G. McGimpsey from the British team, but selectors have a thankless task when their team loses. The United States won by sixteen matches to seven with one halved.

However, there was no doubt that the Club had done its part splendidly. Bill Deedes in "The Telegraph" caught the atmosphere perfectly.

"Thousands were drawn to this two-day event between amateurs and behaved irreproachably. I never saw a policeman, nor a man draining a beer can, nor anyone removing his shirt. There was no chanting.

The boys who marked the players' shots came from a local prep school and had woven into their jerseys: 'Vive ut discas et disce ut vivas'. It is hard to get classier than that. Around the first tee, after lunch, there was a simply delicious aroma recalling the days before Castro so severely injured the Havana tobacco trade.

..... I shall be told that this was an elitist occasion. Indeed it was, and all the better for it."

The Golf Illustrated Gold Vase

This important amateur tournament has been held many times at Sunningdale, starting in 1910, then again in 1914, on which occasion it was won by the former Amateur and Open Champion, Harold Hilton.

After the 1914-18 war it came to Sunningdale in 1921, and in 1930 when it was won by Bobby Jones. His score was 75 + 68 = 143. Among members playing were N.C. Selway, who won the 36 - hole handicap prize with 150 - 2 = 148, R.H. de Montmorency 151, Major S.K. Thorburn 157, and J.S.F. Morrison 157.

After the second war it was at Sunningdale in 1948, and from 1952 it was at the Club for a continuous run of twenty-one years.

In 1952 the tournament was held on the New Course, generally regarded as a tough test of golf. It resulted in the first of two wins for John Langley. In the morning he came in with a fine score of 72; this led the field, which included several other Sunningdale members - Philip Scrutton, Andrew McNair (then Captain of the Club), Gerald Micklem, Leonard Crawley, and Ian Caldwell.

In the afternoon Langley was out in 33, and round in 68, a new amateur record and a fine exhibition of golf. His nearest rival was Dick Chapman, a leading American amateur who had won in 1948. He had two 73s and was six shots behind. John Langley's figures for his 68 were:

```
OUT:  5,  3,  4,  3,  3,  4,  4,  3,  4  = 33
IN:   4,  4,  4,  4,  3,  5,  4,  3,  4  = 35
Total: 68
```

In 1953, again on the New Course, John Langley had a 70 in the morning to lead the field as in the previous year. His short game was particularly good. After lunch he went round in 73 for a total of 143, two strokes ahead of the runner-up, Wing Commander C.H. Beamish. On the last green he had two putts to win the Vase, but struck the first one firmly into the hole.

Later winners were Guy Wolstenholme in 1957, Clive Clark in 1965, Robin Hunter in a triple tie in 1972, and John Davies in 1973 and 1977.

John Langley
- winner Gold Vase 1952.

In 1977 there was a most exciting finish. The Vase was held at Walton Heath, and in the morning John Davies went round the New Course in 69 (par 72). The holder, Allan Brodie, had a 75 on the Old Course (par 73).

In the afternoon Brodie reached the turn (New) in 33, while Davies reached the turn (Old) in 37, his lead thus reduced to two strokes. Brodie made a great effort to retain the Vase by coming home in 34 for a 36-hole total of 142. Davies meanwhile had dropped another shot at the 10th, but then had a marvellous finish with birdies at the 13th, 16th and 17th to end at one under par 72, and a total of 141 to win by one stroke. As a measure of the standard of play of the winner and runner-up the third score by J.K. Tate was 148, seven shots adrift.

In 1993 the Gold Vase was held at Sunningdale. Although conditions were benign the scoring was quite extraordinary.

Bruce Critchley - Gold Vase 1962.
Best round of the day - 68.

There was a tie on 131. Charles Challen (Stoke Poges) aged 18 had a 69 against par 72 on the Old, and a 62 against par 70 on the New - 32 out and 30 in! His fellow Stoke Poges member and Walker Cup player, Van Phillips, had a 68 on the Old and a 63 on the New.

Challen's 62 was a course record. At the start of the day the amateur record stood at 65, set by Michael Lunt in the Vase in 1958. It was first broken by D. Lomas of Woodcote Park with a 64, followed by Phillips with 63, and finally Challen's 62. The amateur record was thus broken three times in one day, with Gary Player's professional record still standing at 64!

Of our Honorary Members, Joe Carr won in 1951, and Michael Bonallack in 1961, 1967, 1968, 1969, 1971 and 1975. A record number of wins, the first five at Sunningdale.

*Michael Bonallack receiving the Gold Vase from the Captain,
John Whitfield in 1971.*

John Davies - winner Gold Vase 1977.

The Qualifying Rounds of the Open Championship at Sunningdale in 1926

Two of the most celebrated rounds of golf were played by R.T. (Bobby) Jones at Sunningdale on the Old Course in Qualifying Rounds for the 1926 Open Championship on Wednesday and Thursday, 16th and 17th June of that year.

The tees were as far back as could be, and several new ones had been specially made for this event. The scratch score was 76. Players were still using hickory-shafted clubs, and the wedge had not yet appeared. These facts should be remembered when considering Bobby Jones' first round score of 66. 33 putts and 33 other strokes - six 4s and three 3s on each nine. Arthur Daley in the New York Times in an obituary article in 1971 wrote that Bobby Jones recognised the round for what it was. He told Daley, "It was as perfect a round as I ever played in my life. Even when I shoot a good round of golf, I doubt that I put six shots exactly where I want, but this was uncanny. I holed one putt of 18 feet, but I didn't have another difficult putt all day. I made two mistakes in the entire round. Both proved trifling. On the short 13th I hooked my tee shot into the bunker, but I blew out to within three feet of the cup. On the 17th I twisted my drive some five feet off the fairway, but the grass wasn't deep and I put my ball on the green. What a round that was!"

The next day he had a 68, which could have been better as several putts failed to drop. On the other hand he ran into difficult problems on the 10th and 11th. On the 10th he hooked his tee shot into heather under the branches of a tree, almost unplayable. Somehow he got the ball onto the fairway, put his next on the green, and only just missed his putt for a four. This was the only five on his card for 36 holes. On the 11th, possibly trying to counter the hook, he pushed his tee shot beyond the trees on the right of the fairway. He had to pitch over the ditch, missing the trees. He got to the edge of the green, put the next one stone dead and the crisis was over. For the remaining holes he was four under fours. His figures were:

16th June OUT: 4, 4, 4, 3, 3, 4, 4, 3, 4 = 33
         IN: 4, 3, 4, 3, 4, 3, 4, 4, 4 = 33 Total: 66
17th June OUT: 4, 4, 4, 4, 4, 4, 4, 3, 4 = 35
         IN: 5, 4, 4, 2, 4, 3, 4, 4, 3 = 33 Total: 68
Total for 36 holes 134

BRITISH OPEN CHAMPIONSHIP, 1926

Two Qualifying Rounds by R. T. Jones (Atlanta Golf Club, U.S.A.)
at Sunningdale Old Course on June 16th and 17th, 1926
Length of Course, 6472 yards

66 and 68

		First Round	
1.	492 Yards.	*DRIVE, SPOON, TWO PUTTS* Spoon shot short and to the right of the pin. Approach putt eighteen inches short of the pin.	4
2.	454 Yards.	*DRIVE, No. 2 IRON, TWO PUTTS* Against the wind. Drive over the road. Iron pin high to right of the pin. Approach putt stone dead.	4
3.	292 Yards.	*DRIVE MASHIE, TWO PUTTS* Drive fifteen yards short and to the right of the bunker guarding green. First putt of three feet missed.	4
4.	152 Yards.	*MASHIE, TWO PUTTS* Mashie short. Run up putt two feet past the hole.	3
5.	417 Yards.	*DRIVE, No. 2 IRON, PUTT* Six yard putt.	3
6.	418 Yards.	*DRIVE, No. 2 IRON, TWO PUTTS* Iron shot four feet past the pin. Should have been another 3.	4
7.	434 Yards.	*DRIVE, No. 2 IRON, TWO PUTTS* Drive fifteen yards short of cross bunker. First putt nine inches past the hole.	4
8.	165 Yards.	*MASHIE, TWO PUTTS* First putt ten yards stone dead.	3
9.	270 Yards.	*DRIVE, MASHIE, TWO PUTTS* Drive pin high just off the green - run up three feet beyond the hole. First putt missed.	4
	3094 Yards.	OUT	33
10.	469 Yards.	*DRIVE, No. 2 IRON, TWO PUTTS* Drive slightly drawn. Iron shot the outstanding shot of the round. Pin high above the hole. First putt stone dead.	4
11.	296 Yards.	*DRIVE, MASHIE, PUTT* Two foot putt.	3
12.	443 Yards.	*DRIVE, No. 2 IRON, TWO PUTTS* Second shot twelve yards short of the pin. First putt stone dead.	4
13.	175 Yards.	*MASHIE, MASHIE, PUTT* First mashie shot cut into bunker on right of the green. The first shot not absolutely in the middle of the club. Recovery from bunker stone dead.	3
14.	503 Yards.	*DRIVE, BRASSIE, TWO PUTTS* A beautiful brassie shot, pin high lay on the edge of the bunker to the left of the green.	4
15.	229 Yards.	*CLEEK, TWO PUTTS* Pin splitter - four feet past the hole - should have been a 2.	3
16.	426 Yards.	*DRIVE, No. 2 IRON, TWO PUTTS* Iron shot not quite as intended, but lay short of the pin. First putt dead.	4
17.	422 Yards.	*DRIVE, MASHIE, TWO PUTTS* Drive cut. Mashie shot from a lucky lie intentionally cut and run right up to the hole.	4
18.	415 Yards.	*DRIVE, MASHIE, TWO PUTTS* Mashie four yards past the hole.	4
	3378 Yards.	HOME	33

	Second Round	
1.	*DRIVE, SPOON, TWO PUTTS* Spoon shot short and to the right of the pin. First putt dead.	4
2.	*DRIVE, No. 2 IRON, RUN UP, PUTT* Iron shot short of the green. Run up two feet past the hole.	4
3.	*DRIVE, NIBLICK, TWO PUTTS* Niblick to clear the bunker guarding the green - three yards past the hole. First putt missed.	4
4.	*MASHIE, RUN UP, TWO PUTTS* First shot over the green. Run up short - over-ran with first putt.	4
5.	*DRIVE, MASHIE, TWO PUTTS* First putt dead.	4
6.	*DRIVE, MASHIE, TWO PUTTS* Mashie shot to the right of pin all the way - finished pin high. First putt missed.	4
7.	*DRIVE, No. 2 IRON, TWO PUTTS* Iron shot pin high on left edge of green. First putt short.	4
8.	*MASHIE, TWO PUTTS* First putt of eight yards missed the hole by two inches.	3
9.	*DRIVE, RUN UP, TWO PUTTS* Drive pin high just off the green to the left. Run up short and to left of pin. First putt missed. Hole played exactly as in previous round.	4
	OUT	35
10.	*DRIVE, NIBLICK, No. 2 IRON, TWO PUTTS* Drive pulled and lay in the wood in bush - well out : perfect iron shot.	5
11.	*DRIVE, NIBLICK, RUN UP, PUTT* Drive cut over the dyke under the trees - lay well - well out. Run up dead.	4
12.	*DRIVE, No. 2 IRON, TWO PUTTS* Iron shot to the right and past the hole. First putt one foot past the hole.	4
13.	*MASHIE, PUTT* Eight yard putt.	2
14.	*DRIVE, BRASSIE, RUN UP, PUTT* Brassie shot over the green. Run back dead.	4
15.	*No. 2 IRON, TWO PUTTS* Another pin splitter. Should have been a 2.	3
16.	*DRIVE, No. 2 IRON, TWO PUTTS* Iron short on left edge of green. First putt nine inches past the hole.	4
17.	*DRIVE, No. 2 IRON, TWO PUTTS* Iron pin high to left of pin.	4
18.	*DRIVE, No. 2 IRON, PUTT* Very long drive. Iron shot four yards short of the pin.	3
	HOME	33

Robt T Jones Jr.

Score card of Qualifying Rounds at Sunningdale.

Bobby Jones - Open Champion 1926.

The Sunningdale Open Foursomes

This popular tournament began in 1934, and from the start it attracted a quality field. The first event was won by Diana Fishwick (later Mrs. Diana Critchley), British Ladies Champion in 1930, and E. Noel Layton. Then Joyce Wethered (later Lady Heathcote Amory), four times British Ladies Champion in the 1920s, and J.S.F. Morrison, D.F.C., Captain of the Club in 1933, won in 1935 and 1936. In 1937 Dai Rees, 1936 British Professional Matchplay Champion, was a winner, followed by Alf Padgham, 1936 Open Champion, on the winning side in 1938.

After the war Max Faulkner won in 1950 before winning the Open in 1951. Tom Haliburton, the professional at Wentworth and Ryder Cup player, won in partnership with Miss Jean Donald (later Mrs. Jean Anderson) in 1951 and 1953.

Philip Scrutton of the home club and Walker Cup player, won in 1952 and 1954 with A. Waters.

Neil Coles, Ryder Cup player, third in the Open in 1961, partnered Ross Whitehead in 1962 to win the first of three victories.

In 1964 there was much excitement and pleasure when the home club partnership of Bruce Critchley and Robin Hunter beat Michael Burgess and Peter Green by 2 and 1 in the final. This was only the second all-amateur partnership to win since the war, the other being Michael Bonallack and Doug Sewell in 1959.

In 1968 there was a remarkable amateur victory by John Davies and Warren Humphreys, respectively aged 20 and not quite 16, when they beat Max Faulkner and Brian Barnes by 6 and 4 in the final. The professionals were conceding three strokes, but the young men were on their way to a below par score when they won. This was the first of three victories for John Davies, and the first of two for Warren Humphreys, the second as a professional.

John Davies and Warren Humphreys winning the Sunningdale Foursomes 1968.

Clive Clark twice won the tournament as a professional, first with Peter Butler in 1974, and then with Michael Hughesdon in 1976 as an all Sunningdale team.

In 1993 Anthony Wall and Steven Webster won a final which will long be remembered by those who witnessed the last nine holes. The winners were each aged 18, the runners-up were aged 18 and 19. The day was bleak, with an unpleasant wind, and from the very back tees the winners took 32 strokes home to the losers 33 to win by one hole - the difference being the putt Anthony Wall holed on the 17th green for yet another birdie.

Looking at the honours board one can detect a change in the tournament. The winners today are still fine players and give much enjoyment to those who turn out to watch. However, the demands of the European Tour, and tournaments in sunny climes in the early part of the year, mean that few of the top professionals can now take part. The tournament has moved on from the time when leading professionals used it as a warm-up at the beginning of the season, but it is still nevertheless a very enjoyable event, as the return of good players year after year testifies.

In 1991 the Club celebrated the 50th Open Foursomes by inviting as many of the past winners and runners-up as could be traced to an informal 18-hole Stableford competition, followed by a reception. The competition was won by Peter Alliss and Pat Garner with a score of 34 points.

The Senior Golfers Society and the Triangular Tournament

This Society of senior golfers over the age of fifty-five was formed in 1926. Similar societies in America and Canada had already been in existence for some years.

R.H. de Montmorency (Sunningdale) was a member of the first committee, and may have been instrumental in bringing the first Triangular International Tournament to Sunningdale. An invitation to the Americans and Canadians to take part in such a tournament was one of the first acts of the Society, and a match duly took place on 6th and 7th July, 1927 at Sunningdale. Teams were fourteen a side and the match was played by a series of three balls and three-ball sixsomes - all against all. Lord Derby, one of the Vice-Presidents of the Society, donated the Derby Cup.

Ages ranged from 55 to 77, the oldest player being an American, General J.E. Smith, standing straight as a gun barrel and hitting the ball a good 180 yards. He and his partner were one of two American couples to gain the maximum of four points in the foursomes. The format of the play made scoring somewhat complicated, one observer commenting that the player needed to be an accountant as well as a golfer. In the end the British took the Cup, with the U.S.A. second and Canada third.

The Triangular Tournament 1927 - Joshua Crane putting.

In 1977 the Golden Jubilee of the Triangular Tournament was held at Sunningdale. The U.S.A. won the team event, and David Blair of the British team won the medal event with 72. A dinner was held in the Club at the end of the Tournament when the cup was presented to the Americans by the Earl of Derby M.C..

This match is played every two years in turn in Britain, America and Canada.

Sunningdale has been closely associated with the Seniors. Major Guy Bennett, Secretary of the Club before the second war became Secretary of the Seniors in 1945. James Moir, Captain of the Club in 1946 and 1947, took over from Guy Bennett in 1952. Captain F.B. ("Frankie") Lloyd O.B.E., R.N., who was Captain of Sunningdale in 1963 served as Secretary of the Seniors from 1960 to 1974 and was later Captain of the Society.

More recently, Graham Young, Captain of the Club in 1983, initiated a match with the Seniors which has proved popular both with the Club and the Seniors.

The Bowmaker Tournament

This tournament was held at the Club from 1958 to 1969. The format was two amateurs playing with a professional in each team. The amateurs played off handicap and the best ball of the three players counted at each hole. The professional was also playing for an individual money prize, and amongst the winners were Open Champions A.D. Locke, P.W. Thomson, R.J. Charles and K.D.G. Nagle.

The Colgate European Women's Open Championship

An approach by David Foster, a member of the Club, and President and Chief Executive Officer of Colgate Palmolive Ltd., brought this Championship to the Club in 1974, and for five years thereafter.

Laura Baugh

The first tournament was over 54 holes. 40 American women professionals and some 50 European women amateurs and professionals were in the field. It was the first time that such an event with players of this calibre had taken place in this country.

128

With fine weather, mini-skirts, and scores in the low
seventies, there was a garden party atmosphere at the Club,
and many members were able to enjoy playing in the pro-am
before the main event. The Championship was won by Judy
Rankin with a three round total of 218. She was much helped
by her caddie, Ron Mullens, one of the best known
Sunningdale caddies and a good golfer himself. Mrs. Rankin
asked him at one point if he would like a trip to the States, to
which he replied, "Are there any horses?" He was well known
for liking a flutter, and indeed had backed Judy with £5 to win
at 12 to 1.

Of the six championships played at the Club, all except the
first were over 72 holes; two were won by Judy Rankin and two
by Nancy Lopez. The remaining two were won by Donna
Young and Chako Higuchi.

Many members were sorry to see this annual "Ascot of Golf"
come to an end when Colgate withdrew their sponsorship.

Judy Rankin

Nancy Lopez

The European Open Championship

This tournament was held at Sunningdale from 1982 to 1986 and then alternately with Walton Heath until 1992. National Panasonic were the sponsors for all except the first and last year when the sponsorship was taken over by General Accident. The list of winners includes many well-known names such as Bernhard Langer, Greg Norman, Ian Woosnam and Nick Faldo.

Considering the distance such players hit the ball the strict par of the Old course, even from the championship tees, is for them 68, so a four-round total of 272 would represent level par. That being the case, one can say the Old course held its own during these championships. The first one was won by Manuel Pinero with a score of 266, but the next was won by Isao Aoki on 274. Only nine players on that occasion were below 280 for the four rounds.

In later years the winners had lower scores, the lowest being Ian Woosnam on 260 in 1988, and Nick Faldo on 262 in 1992, but the fact remains that the bulk of the field had much higher scores. From the sponsor's point of view it is convenient to take the par of 70 as the yardstick, but even then in 1990, for example, 74 players missed the 36-hole cut at 142, 16 took more than 280 for the four rounds, and only 10 of the remaining 53 were 272 or better. The winner that year was Peter Senior on 267.

The tournament has now gone to a new venue. Although members were pleased to have the opportunity of seeing leading professionals play the Old course, there was a growing feeling that it was becoming increasingly difficult to provide the facilities for the modern tournament "circus". The grandstands, the hospitality units, the car parking, the inevitable disruption to club life, and not least the risk of serious damage to the course and its surroundings in the event of bad weather, all rather indicated it was unlikely the Club would host such a large tournament in future.

In 1993, 1994 and 1995 the Club was host to the Forte P.G.A. Seniors' Tournament, and in 1995 was host to the first British Mid-Amateur Championship. The general feeling is that the size of such events more suits the Club.

Manuel Pinero

Bernhard Langer

Nick Faldo

Greg Norman

131

Club Competitions

The principal Club competitions are the scratch Spring and Autumn Gold Medals, the Longman Cup for the best combined score in those medals, the Connaught Cup for the best combined handicap score in the Spring and Autumn handicap competitions, the Scratch Match Play Championship, and the Founders' Singles and Foursomes Cups.

Photographs of the Honours Board for these and other club competitions are at the end of the book, but the Spring and Autumn Gold Medals deserve a special mention. Not surprisingly, many of the winners have featured in the sections on the Amateur Championship, the Walker Cup and the Gold Vase.

In fact the first winner of the Autumn Medal in 1902 was the Hon. Osmund Scott, who won again in 1904, and was runner-up in the Amateur Championship of 1905 at Prestwick.

C.C. Lingen, who won the Spring Medal in 1906 was that year a finalist in the Amateur Championship.

Those who have won a number of medals include H.E. Taylor, who won five Spring Medals from 1909 to 1913 inclusive. He also won the Autumn Medal in 1912. His five consecutive wins have never been equalled.

Captain R.H. Jobson, M.C. had three Spring Medals to his credit, and folklore has it that on one occasion on the Sunningdale Ladies course he had seventeen threes, drove the last green, and then three-putted.

Captain S.K. Thorburn, M.C. collected five medals between 1925 and 1933, the first two as Captain, and last three as Major.

The Hartley brothers, both Walker Cup players, were both medal winners. Rex won three Spring Medals in the 1930s, and Lister won the Autumn Medal in 1934.

D.H. Kyle, Scottish International, Walker Cup player and Captain of Sunningdale in 1936, won a total of five medals.

Leonard Crawley won eight medals, three before the last war and five afterwards, a record which has now been surpassed by Robin Hunter.

Robert Sweeney, Amateur Champion in 1937, won the Spring Medal in 1948 and the Autumn Medal in 1969, 21 years later. According to the honours board he was awarded his D.F.C. in the interim, but this is surely an error and should apply to his win in 1948 also.

In the early 1950s Gerald Micklem collected three medals, and John Langley won the Spring Medal in 1952 and 1953, the same years that he won the Gold Vase.

Gerald Micklem - English Champion 1953.

David Frame won five medals between 1956 and 1960, four in the spring and one in the autumn.

In the 1960s and 1970s Robin Hunter, a Scottish International, won a total of nine medals - the current record. He and Bruce Critchley (five medals), Leslie McClue (five medals) and Ian Caldwell (three medals plus a later one in 1981) dominated the scene.

Later in the 1970s and 1980s John Davies won six medals, and Michael Hughesdon won seven, plus another in 1992, drawing level with Leonard Crawley's tally of eight. His score of 66 in the 1987 Autumn Medal equalled the previous lowest score of Gerald Bristowe in 1955, although Michael was playing over a longer course.

Ted Dexter, the England cricket captain, who might otherwise have been a Walker Cup player, and perhaps a contender for the Amateur Championship, won the Spring Medal in 1969, 1984, and 1987. He also won the President's Putter of the Oxford and Cambridge Golfing Society in 1983 and 1985.

Rupert Kellock, a former officer in the Greenjackets, has started to accumulate medals. He won the Autumn Medal in 1988 and 1989, and the Spring in 1991. He also won the Founders' Singles in 1989. At his first attempt he won the Spring Medal of the Royal and Ancient Golf Club of St. Andrews, and has won a number of top events at Royal St. George's. There may well be some more Sunningdale medals to come.

The Founders Singles and Foursomes, both match-play events, have produced many exciting finishes. There was a unique family occasion in May, 1971, when the final of the Singles was contested by two brothers. The older brother, E.D.S. Aldrich-Blake (handicap 9) beat his younger brother, A.De C. Aldrich-Blake (handicap 6) - a former Blue - by 1 hole.

On the 18th tee E.D.S. was one up, but after a hooked drive and another shot was still not on the green, whereas his brother, being on for two, walked over to the first tee and put his bag down, clearly indicating he was sure the match would go down the 19th. E.D.S. said afterwards that he was so incensed by this that it increased his determination; he put his third shot dead and won the match.

Club Matches

The Club has played matches against Oxford and Cambridge Universities since its early days, and more recently against London. On most occasions the Club has turned out a strong side, and has won the matches fairly comfortably. With players such as Cyril Tolley, Leonard Crawley, the Hartley brothers, Eustace Storey, Gerald Micklem, John Langley, Ian Caldwell, Bruce Critchley, Ted Dexter and John Davies, the Club sides have presented a formidable task for the undergraduates.

At a somewhat lower level many enjoyable matches have been played against sides such as the Surrey Police, the

Greenjackets, the Parliamentary Golfing Society, the Senior Golfers Society, the Army Officers Golfing Society and the Thames Valley Police.

One particular match, which sadly is no longer played, is worthy of a special mention - Sunningdale versus Woking. This was a two-day eight-a-side foursomes match over a weekend, with 36 holes at one of the Clubs on the first day, and 36 holes at the other Club on the second day.

The match was already well established before the First World War, and was clearly a major event in both Clubs' calendars. In a newspaper report of the match in June, 1912, entitled "The Best Inter-Club Match", A.C.M. Croome wrote: "Having played for one Club or the other in past years, we would allow no engagement less pressing than our own funerals to prevent us from again taking the place offered to us, not primarily for personal gratification, although the pleasantness of the games becomes after a decent interval the salient feature in our recollection of them. While we are actually going our rounds we thirst for blood. That the much desired liquid flows in the veins of men who are among our closest friends everywhere except on two golf courses, makes the slaking of that thirst poignantly satisfactory. It is a condition of intimate friendship that the parties, while agreeing on their general outlook on life, should differ completely on one important point. Of all the men who have with any regularity represented either Woking or Sunningdale, only one is a member of both clubs. Each and all of the others has at some time stated either that Woking course is short and tricky, or that Sunningdale is wide and in places blind. The rivalry implied by the fact produces further comparisions of putting greens, bunkers, rough - in extreme cases even of luncheon."

The quality of the players was high, as can be seen from a report in June, 1927. In the Sunningdale team were E.B.H. Blackwell, E.R. Campbell, and H. Gardiner-Hill; for Woking, R.H. Wethered and B. Darwin.

The match was briefly revived after the Second World War, but times were changing and it became increasingly difficult to find eight players for each side, of sufficient calibre, to commit themselves to a two-day match. With regrets on both sides it was abandoned.

Many other matches of interest have taken place at the Club. In May, 1937, four South African amateur golfers played a match against a Sunningdale team. In retrospect it is of particular interest that one of the South Africans was Arthur D'Arcy (Bobby) Locke before he turned professional and won four Open Championships. His singles match was against Leonard Crawley, who was out in 32 and turned two up. Locke was out in 34, and level fours thereafter, but Crawley became three up at the 15th and ran out the winner by three and two.

FOURSOMES

Sunningdale

D.H. Kyle & T.A. Bourn	0
L.G. Crawley & Major S.K. Thorburn (3/2)	<u>1</u>
	1

South Africa

A.D'A. Locke & C.E. Olander	1
F.O.L. Agg & O. Hayes	<u>0</u>
	1

SINGLES

L.G. Crawley (3 & 2)	1	A.D'A. Locke	0
D.H. Kyle (3 & 2)	1	C.E. Olander	0
T.A. Bourn	0	O. Hayes (2 & 1)	1
Major S.K. Thorburn	<u>0</u>	F.O.L. Agg (2 & 1)	<u>1</u>
Total	2		2

No doubt there will be other interesting matches of one kind or another in the next century, but perhaps the foregoing has given the flavour of some of those which have taken place in this one.

* * * * *

There have been, and are, many good golfers in the Club who are not mentioned in this chapter, but with such a large number of distinguished players a line had to be drawn. Whilst the chapter thus covers mainly those with national or international honours, the reputation of the Club for a high standard of play rests not only on them, but also on others who have played County golf, and indeed won County Championships, and on the more than 80 members in Category one (handicaps of five or less); not forgetting numerous others of higher but competitive handicaps.

Dr. W.G. Grace at Sunningdale, 1906.

Members who have played in the International, National, and County events, with a record of some of their principal achievements:

Harry Bentley
Walker Cup 1934 and 1938
French Open Amateur 1931 and 1932
German Open Amateur 1933
English Amateur 1936
Italian Open Amateur 1954

T. (Dale) Bourn
Runner-up Amateur Championship 1933
French Amateur 1928
President's Putter 1930
English Amateur 1930

Tim Coltart
Sussex under 23 Championship 1960
(Allan Powell scratch medal)

Nino Brito e Cuna (Visconde de Pereira Machado)
Portuguese Open Amateur 1962, 1963, 1979 and 1980
Portuguese Amateur 1959, 1960 and 1967
Portuguese Eisenhower Trophy Team 1960, 1970, 1980
Portuguese St. Andrews Trophy Team 1968 and 1972

Ian Caldwell
Walker Cup 1951 and 1955
International v France 1949
Great Britain v Commonwealth 1954
Great Britain v Europe 1955 and 1972
English Home International 1950 to 1957 inclusive and 1961
English Amateur 1961
Prince of Wales Challenge Cup 1950, 1951 and 1952
Antlers, Royal Mid-Surrey 1951
Boyd Quaich 1954
Kent Cob 1957
Bishop Bowl 1957
Winkley Smith Cup 1963
English Boys (Carris Trophy) 1947 and 1948
English Boys v Scotland 1948
Surrey Amateur 1961
English Seniors Amateur Open 1987 and 1990

W.T. (Tommie) Campbell
Longest recorded drive - 392 yards at Foxrock Golf Club, Co.
Dublin, July 1964. In the Guinness Book of Records for 26
consecutive years.

John Carr
Irish International 1981, 1982, 1983

Philip Carr
Worplesdon Mixed Foursomes 1995

Roddy Carr
Walker Cup 1971
Irish International 1970 and 1971
European Team Championship 1971
Antlers, Royal Mid-Surrey 1969
East of Ireland Amateur 1970
West of Ireland Amateur 1971
Leading Amateur South African Open 1971
Turned Professional autumn 1971

Harry Colt (*Captain of Sunningdale 1924*)
Semi-finalist Amateur Championship 1906
English International 1908

Leonard Crawley
Walker Cup 1932, 1934, 1938 and 1947
English Amateur 1931, runner-up 1934 and 1937
President's Putter 1932, 1947, 1951 and 1952
Runner up French Open 1937

Brigadier-General A.C. Critchley
French Open Amateur 1933
Belgian Open Amateur 1938
Surrey Amateur 1938

Bruce Critchley
Walker Cup 1969
Semi-finalist Amateur Championship 1970
European Team Championship 1969
Great Britain v Europe 1970
English International 1962, 1969 and 1970
Worplesdon Mixed Foursomes 1961
Sunningdale Foursomes 1964
Hampshire Hog 1969
Surrey Amateur 1969
Antlers, Royal Mid-Surrey 1974

John Davies
Walker Cup 1973, 1975, 1977 and 1979
Runner-up Amateur Championship 1976
English International 1969 to 1974 inclusive and 1978
Runner-up English Amateur 1971 and 1976
Runner-up English Amateur Stroke Play 1977
Berkshire Trophy 1969 and 1971 (tie)
Royal St. George's Challenge Cup 1972 to 1977 inclusive
Gold Vase 1973 and 1977
Sunningdale Foursomes 1968 and 1972
Antlers, Royal Mid-Surrey 1969, 1975 and 1977
Prince of Wales Cup 1975
Berkhamstead Trophy 1976, 1978 and 1979
Lagonda Trophy 1976 and 1978
Surrey Amateur 1971, 1972 and 1977

Derek Davies (*Captain of Sunningdale, 1986*)
Hong Kong Amateur 1949
Malayan Amateur 1950

M.D. Dawson
Scottish International 1963, 1965, 1966

Martin Devetta
Middlesex Amateur 1973, runner-up 1968
Surrey Amateur 1979
Fathers and Sons, West Hill 1967
Sunningdale Foursomes 1983
John Cross Bowl, Worplesdon 1985

E.R. (Ted) Dexter
President's Putter 1983 and 1985
Prince of Wales Cup 1978

Charles Dugan-Chapman
Portuguese Open Amateur 1960; runner-up 1963

Colonel A.A. Duncan
Amateur Championship runner-up 1939
Welsh Amateur 1938 to 1948, and 1952 to 1954
Walker Cup non-playing Captain 1953
Welsh International 1933, 1934, 1936, 1938 and 1947 to 1959
President's Putter 1948 and 1958

George Duncan
Welsh International 1952 to 1958
Great Britain & Ireland v Rest of Europe 1956
President's Putter 1956 and 1974
Welsh Amateur semi-finalist 1956
Worplesdon Mixed Foursomes - runner-up 1955

John de Forest (Count John de Bendern)
Walker Cup 1932
Amateur Championship 1932, runner-up 1931
Surrey Amateur 1949

David Frame
Walker Cup 1961
Surrey Amateur 1959
Worplesdon Mixed Foursomes 1971
Hampshire Hog 1971

Hon. Osmund Scott
Runner-up Amateur Championship 1905

Philip Scrutton
Walker Cup 1955 and 1957
English Open Amateur Strokeplay 1952, 1954 and 1955
Berkshire Trophy 1950, 1951 and 1952
Brabazon Trophy 1952, 1954 and 1955
Prince of Wales Challenge Cup 1956
Royal St. George's Challenge Cup 1949, 1951, 1955, 1957, and 1958
Surrey Amateur 1951

E.R. Smirke
Semi-finalist Amateur Championship 1906

Eustace Storey
Runner-up Amateur Championship 1924
Walker Cup 1924, 1926 and 1928
President's Putter 1926 (tie)
Leading Amateur Open Championship 1938

Bruce Streather *(Captain of Sunningdale, 1996)*
Finney Shield (Midland Amateur Foursomes) 1973
Cork Scratch Cup (S.W. Ireland) 1974
Highgate Open Amateur 1985
Lord Warden Cup (Rye) 1986

Ian Stungo
Middlesex Amateur 1976, 1978 and 1979

Jeremy Sutherland Pilch
Irish Universities 1966
Belgian Open Amateur 1968
Iranian Open 1976

Robert Sweeney Jr.
Amateur Championship 1937; runner-up 1946
Gold Vase 1937
Runner-up U.S. Amateur 1954 (losing to Arnold Palmer by one hole)

Cyril Tolley
Amateur Championship 1920 and 1929
Walker Cup 1922, 1923, 1924, 1926, 1930 and 1934
French Open Championship 1924 and 1928
Gold Vase 1923, 1926 (tie), and 1928
President's Putter 1938
Captain, Royal & Ancient Golf Club of St. Andrews 1948

John Tullis *(Captain of Sunningdale, 1985)*
Berks, Bucks & Oxon Amateur 1959

Anthony Wall
Gold Vase 1995
Sunningdale Foursomes 1994
Surrey Amateur 1992
Turned Professional late 1995

Lt. General Sir Christopher Wallace
Army Champion 1970 and 1971
Army Team 1968 to 1982

Andrew Wilmot
British Universities Strokeplay 1979
British Universities Matchplay 1979
Berks, Bucks & Oxon Colts 1979
Berks, Bucks & Oxon Foursomes 1978 and 1980

Guy Wolstenholme
Walker Cup 1957 and 1959
English Amateur 1956 and 1959
Gold Vase 1957
English Open Amateur Strokeplay 1960
Turned Professional 1960
British P.G.A. Close Championship 1966
Southern Professional 1961
Danish Open 1967
Kenya Open 1967
Dutch Open 1969
Australian Seniors 1981
England in World Cup 1965

Associate Lady Members

Mrs. Louisa Abrahams (Lady Abrahams) *(Lady Captain Sunningdale 1964)*
Czech Ladies Open 1938

Mrs. Carole Caldwell *(Lady Captain Sunningdale, 1984)*
Curtis Cup 1978 and 1980
Vagliano Trophy 1973
English International 1973 to 1978
Canadian Ladies Foursomes 1978
Portuguese Ladies Champion 1980
Newmark Avia International 1973
Avia Foursomes 1974
Hampshire Rose 1973 and 1984
Roehampton Gold Cup 1973, 1975 and 1978
South-East Champion 1973, 1978 and 1981
Worplesdon Mixed Foursomes 1995
Kent Ladies Champion 1970, 1975, 1977, 1986, 1990, 1993 and 1995
Berkshire Ladies Champion 1982
Critchley Salver 1974 and 1992
British Team Tour of Canada 1973 (playing Captain)

Mrs. Joan Cowper
Finalist British Girls Championship 1935 and 1938
Northern Champion 1939
Finalist Worplesdon Mixed Foursomes 1946 (with Henry Longhurst)
Cheshire Champion 1947, 1948 and 1949
Ladies London Foursomes 1950, 1951 and 1955
Surrey Ladies County Golf Captain 1955

Mrs. Diana Critchley (Miss Diana Fishwick) *(Lady Captain Sunningdale, 1954)*
Curtis Cup 1932 and 1934 (non playing Captain 1950)
British Girls Open 1927 and 1928
British Ladies 1930
English Ladies 1932 and 1949
French Ladies Open 1932; runner-up 1946
Florida West Coast 1933
German Ladies Open 1936 and 1938
Belgian Ladies Open 1938
Dutch International Ladies 1946

CHAPTER EIGHT

Epilogue

Gerald Micklem C.B.E 1911 - 1988

Gerald Micklem was educated at Winchester and Oxford, where he gained a Blue for golf in the thirties. During the war he served in the Grenadier Guards; for a time afterwards he was a stockbroker, but when his father died he retired and became involved wholly with the game of golf in all its aspects.

His playing record is given at the end of the previous chapter, but a particular mention should be made of his two English Championships. In the first in 1947 at Ganton he won by one hole against Charlie Stowe. In the second in 1953 at Royal Birkdale he defeated Ronnie White by two and one. At that time Ronnie White was considered to be the best amateur in the country; he was also a member of Birkdale and was the favourite to win.

In the morning round White was impressive through the green, but Micklem had the edge on the greens. White ended the round one up, being round in 72 to Micklem's 73. In the afternoon both men were playing excellent golf, and White remained one up at the turn, although his putting was giving him problems. Micklem, however, was putting superbly and on the back nine, according to Tom Scott in Golf Illustrated, "at every hole he was stone dead or actually in the hole from distances varying from 30 yards to 9 feet". With a winning putt at the 14th Gerald squared the match, and with another at the 15th went one up. The 16th was halved, and at the 17th Gerald hit a glorious wooden club shot close to the pin. White failed to match it, and the Championship was Gerald's.

In his latter years Gerald devoted himself to the administration of the game, serving on the principal committees of the Royal and Ancient, of which he was Captain in 1968. He played a major part in re-establishing Sunningdale as a leading inland Club after the war, and was Captain in 1960.

He was invariably consulted when a problem arose over the Rules of Golf, and was a constant source of advice and hospitality to young players, and others. Every year he supervised the entry and draw for the Sunningdale Foursomes, together with Cecil Elliott.

He was much involved with the move to adopt the larger, American size, ball, and most important of all with the raising of the Open Championship to the level of world-wide prestige it now enjoys.

He was President of the Oxford and Cambridge Golfing Society, and received awards from the British Golf Writers, as well as the Bobby Jones and Walter Hagen awards in the United States.

He was President of Sunningdale from 1984 until his death in 1988.

Harry Shapland Colt

Harry Colt's place in the history of the Club as its first Secretary has been recorded in the early part of this book. Reference was made to his increasing activity as a golf course architect, and that this eventually led to his retirement as Secretary, although he continued to advise the Club on matters to do with the green for some years.

As a golf course architect he developed an international reputation, and laid out or modified many of the courses well known to members of Sunningdale, as well as the New Course itself.

Harry Colt was born in 1869 and died in 1951. He won a Blue for golf at Cambridge, and by 1893 had a scratch handicap. He was a member of the Royal and Ancient, and was the winner of the Jubilee Vase (match-play singles) in 1891 and 1893.

He was mainly responsible for the initial layout of Rye, and was its first Captain in 1894. He is recorded as winning the final medal of that year with $81 + 1 = 82$.

Well-known courses designed by him in the South of England are Blackmoor, Brockenhurst Manor, Calcot Park, Camberley Heath, Cuddington, Moor Park, St. George's Hill,

Stoke Poges, Swinley Forest, Tandridge, Wentworth (East and West) and Royal Worlington.

Colt and his partners, Hugh Alison, Alister MacKenzie and John Morrison were involved in the design or modification of numerous other courses in the British Isles, and in many countries overseas.

Harry Colt was appointed an Honorary Member of Sunningdale in 1918, and was Captain in 1924.

Sunningdale and the R & A

Sunningdale has a strong connection with the Royal and Ancient Golf Club of St. Andrews. There are upwards of 80 members of Sunningdale who are also members of the R & A.

Over the years many members have been successful in the annual spring and autumn meetings, and quite a few have served on club committees. In the recent past, Johnny Boardman, the late Ted Harker, and Nicholas Royds served on the important Championship Committee; the Open and Amateur Championships are two of its principal responsibilities. Johnny and Nicholas have also served on the Rules Committee, as has Maurice Baird, and in 1995 Johnny became a member of the General Committee. (1998/99 Deputy Chairman).

Some prominent members of Sunningdale have been Captains of the R & A. The first was H.R.H. The Prince of Wales in 1922, followed by Angus Hambro, H.R.H. The Duke of York, Cyril Tolley, Dr. Harold Gardiner-Hill, John Beck, Gerald Micklem and The Rt. Hon. Lord Griffiths. Lord Griffiths has the rare distinction of having also been president of the Marylebone Cricket Club, and in 1994 R. & A members of Sunningdale held a dinner in the Clubhouse in his honour.

Of our Honorary Members, Joe Carr was Captain of the R & A in 1991, and Michael Bonallack is the Secretary, the latter being knighted in 1998 for his services to golf.

All in all, it is doubtful whether any other club has stronger ties with the R & A.

Sunningdale Seniors

In recent years in many clubs there have grown up groups of older members, mostly retired, who meet informally once or twice a week to play golf. These groups are known in their clubs by various soubriquets such as "Dad's Army"; Sunningdale members call themselves simply Sunningdale Seniors.

The number of members who participate has grown rapidly, no doubt as a result of members retiring earlier and living longer. There are now some fifty who take part in these games and matches.

In 1993 Rab McEwan and Tim Kelly took the initiative to arrange some matches with other clubs. With the Committee's consent three home and three away, matches were organised. The clubs were Worplesdon, North Hants, West Hill, Hankley Common, Liphook and Woking, all of which had been playing such matches for some time past. Since then, additional matches have been arranged with West Sussex, Walton Heath, New Zealand, St. George's Hill, and in 1996 against our own Associate Lady Members.

These are convivial occasions, much enjoyed by the participants, as indeed are the usual weekly games.

The Membership

"At Sunningdale the great are treated as unremarkable. That is why they come."

(Jimmy Sheridan)

Apart from the good golfers who have always been attracted to Sunningdale, many members are, or have been, eminent in their everyday lives.

It would be invidious, and indeed impracticable to attempt to compile a list of such members. Suffice it to say, the past and present membership includes High Court Judges, chairmen of major industrial companies such as Shell and I.C.I., and of Lloyd's of London, Royal Navy Captains, Army Generals, senior Royal Air Force officers, Ambassadors, and leading barristers and actors.

Past members include Somerset Maugham, who was elected on 28 June, 1913, Lord Brabazon of Tara, Terence Rattigan, and Halford Hewitt, who gave his name to the ever-popular foursomes tournament. Sheridan records in his book that he was a somewhat irascible character on the golf course with a tendency to throw clubs, and that he was also a stickler for replacing divots. One day Bert Chapman, a long-serving greenkeeper mentioned in chapter one, was caddying for him. Hewitt hit a bad shot, threw a club, and said "Pick it up, Bert, and don't forget to replace the divot." To which Chapman replied, "I can't do it all, sir. Either you put back the divot, and I'll get the club or vice versa. I'm not doing both!"

It is of interest that some of the second round matches of the first Halford Hewitt Tournament in 1924 took place at Sunningdale, in the days when rounds were played at various clubs; Winchester beat Highgate 5-0, and Rugby had a walk-over against Beaumont. Eton beat Winchester 4-1 in the final at Addington, R.H. Jobson, M.C. of Sunningdale being in the winning team.

Another figure from the past, recorded by Sheridan, was Mr. Vivian Cornelius. He had a good lunch, and when three members were looking for a fourth he joined them. He hit a long drive off the first tee, then had an "air-shot", and holed out with his third. His partners thought his second shot was a practice swing, and that he had holed out in two!

John Morrison D.F.C., who was Captain of the Club in 1933, was a Carthusian who played regularly, and successfully, with Henry Longhurst in the Halford Hewitt. A large, strong, man, he was awarded a Blue at Cambridge for football before the first world war and Blues for cricket and golf when he went back to the university afterwards.

In the twenties and thirties he joined Harry Colt as a golf course architect, being responsible for the New Course alterations in 1937/38. He played regularly in the Amateur Championship, won the Belgian Amateur in 1929, and is credited with instigating the Sunningdale Foursomes in 1934; a tournament which he won with Joyce Wethered in 1935 and 1936.

In recent times the Club suffered a sad loss when Richard ("Rocky") Shaw died suddenly when in office as Captain in

1995. His father had been Captain in 1965, and Rocky was particularly proud to have followed his father in that office. Apart from any other claims to fame, Rocky won the Grand National in 1984 with "Hello Dandy", and for a while the trophy resided in the Clubhouse.

This random collection of anecdotes gives but a brief glimpse of the many colourful members the Club has been fortunate to have in its first hundred years.

A Celebration Dinner

In 1994 and 1995 the Curtis Cup (1994), the Walker Cup (1995) and the Ryder Cup (1995) were all won by Great Britain and Ireland teams.

In December, 1995, a Dinner was held in the Club in honour of the teams, as a result of an initiative by Ian Caldwell. The evening was universally acclaimed a great success.

Bruce Streather, as acting Captain, proposed the toast of International Golf and the Guests. Joe Carr proposed the toast of Sunningdale Golf Club on behalf of the Guests.

The guest list, in alphabetical order, was as follows:

Mrs. Elizabeth Boatman	Captain of the winning Curtis Cup Team
Mr Clive Brown	Captain of the winning Walker Cup Team
Mr. Joe Carr	Former Captain of the Walker Cup Team Former Walker Cup Player Former Amateur Champion
Mrs. Carole Caldwell	Former Curtis Cup Player
Mr. Ian Caldwell	Former Walker Cup Player Former English Amateur Champion
Mr. Bruce Critchley	Former Walker Cup Player

Mr Jodi Flanagan	Walker Cup Player The Irish Amateur Champion
Mr. Mark Foster	Walker Cup Player The English Amateur Champion
Mr. Stephen Gallacher	Walker Cup Player The Scottish Amateur Champion
Mr. Bernard Gallacher	Captain of the winning Ryder Cup Team Former Ryder Cup Player
Mrs. Julie Hall	Curtis Cup Player The British Ladies Amateur Champion The English Ladies Amateur Champion
Mrs. Marley Harris	Former Curtis Cup Player Former British Ladies Amateur Champion
Mr. Bernard Hunt	Captain of the P.G.A. Former Ryder Cup Player
Mr. George O'Grady	European Tour
Dr. Barbara Roberts	The President of the L.G.U.
Mr. Gordon Sherry	Walker Cup Player The Amateur Champion
Miss Kirsty Speak	Curtis Cup Player Former British Ladies Amateur Champion
Mr. Michael Williams	Daily Telegraph Correspondent

154

Finis

For many years a long, semi-circular seat was behind the 10th green of the Old Course, close to the Halfway Hut. The seat was unfortunately destroyed by fire, but has since been replaced. Carved in the wooden back of the seat is the following inscription.

Earth has so many ways of being fair
Its sweet young spring, its summer clothed in light
Its regal autumn trailing into sight
as summer wafts her last kiss on the air.

A fitting note on which to end this book.

Appendix 1

SUNNINGDALE GOLF CLUB

RIDGE MOUNT,
SUNNINGDALE
JULY 21ST, 1900

Dear Sir,

The Tenders for the Club House have now been received, and the lowest is so much above the estimate, that the Committee do not feel justified in accepting any Tender without consulting the Debenture-holders as to the best course to pursue. The plans have been cut down to as low a point as is possible for the convenience of the probable number of Members, and if they are to be carried out, a further sum of £3,000 must be raised.

The following Resolution will be proposed at a Meeting of Debenture-holders, to be held on Monday, July 30th, at the Café Monico, London at 3 o'clock in the afternoon.

The Committee will be obliged if all Debenture-holders who cannot attend the Meeting will sign the enclosed form of Proxy and return it to me, so that the building may be commenced without any further delay.

Yours truly,

M. ERSKINE

SUNNINGDALE GOLF CLUB

RESOLUTION

To be proposed at the MEETING OF DEBENTURE HOLDERS, on MONDAY, JULY 30th, at THREE o'clock at the CAFÉ MONICO, LONDON:-

"That the Committee be, and they are hereby authorised, to make such arrangements as they may in their discretion think fit for raising the further sum of £3,000 for the purposes of the Club upon such terms and in such manner, and whether in priority to the existing Debentures or otherwise, as they may decide, and that the Trustees of the Club, in accordance with the provisions of Rule XXII., be and they are hereby authorised, subject to the approval of the Committee, to execute such instruments as may be necessary for giving effect to such arrangements."

Appendix 2

SUNNINGDALE GOLF CLUB

Ridge Mount,
Sunningdale
April 19th, 1901

Dear Sir,

On August 4th of last year, at a meeting of the Founders specially called for the purpose, power was given to the Committee by the unanimous vote of those present, to borrow a sum of £3,000 in such manner as they should see fit, such loan to rank before the existing Founders' Shares, for the following reasons:-

In the original scheme the cost of the Club House was estimated at £5,000 only, but as the building lease of 99 years provides that a substantial brick structure shall be built, and as it is evident that the Club House will have to accommodate 500 Members at the least, the Committee, after amending the original plans, could not see their way to cut them down any further, and the lowest tender received (and accepted) was £7,699. The other absolutely necessary item is the piping, etc., for the supply of water to the Greens, which will cost at least £500.

From the estimates of receipts and payments both on capital account and working expenditure account sent herewith, it will be seen that £3,000 is hardly sufficient, and it may be necessary to borrow £4,000.

The Committee are pleased to be able to report that the course is progressing very favourably and that there is little doubt it will be ready for play early in October. The Club House is now roofed in and there will be no difficulty in having it ready in good time for the opening of the Club.

Although no money has been spent in advertising, 424 Members have already been elected, and the full number of 500 will certainly be complete before the course is ready for play. As there is a reasonable probability of further and increased entrance fees being received, and as there will be always a large amount paid in as subscriptions at the beginning of each year, the Committee do not anticipate any difficulty in carrying on the Club, with a little assistance from their bankers towards the close of the year.

It is hoped you will be able to attend the meeting on 29th April (notice of which is enclosed), but in the event of your being unable to do so, the Committee will feel much obliged by your kindly filling up the Proxy Form sent herewith, and returning it in the envelope enclosed for that purpose, so that your vote may not be lost.

I am yours truly,

M. ERSKINE
Secretary

By Order of the Committee

SUNNINGDALE GOLF CLUB

ESTIMATED CAPITAL ACCOUNT

DR.	£	s.	d.	CR.	£	s.	d.
To Founders' Debentures-				By W. Park's Contract for making the Links	3,800	0	0
				By Martin Wells, for building the Club House and extras	8,000	0	0
Paid 7,000 0 0				By Quantity Surveyor	96	5	0
Due 1st May 1,000 0 0				By Architect (out-pockets only, no charge for personal service)	200	0	0
Due 1st July 1,000 0 0				By Water Pipes for Greens	500	0	0
Due 1st Aug. 1,000 0 0	10,000	0	0	By Fencing, Gardener's Work, making Roads, Footpaths, etc	200	0	0
To Proposed issue of 100 £50 First Mortgage 4% Debentures, £40 Paid on Club House	4,000	0	0	By Lockers	250	0	0
To 200 Entrance Fees of £5 5s.	1,050	0	0	By Furniture	1,000	0	0
				By Provision for wiring for Electric Lighting	100	0	0
				By Secretary's Salary 15 months	125	0	0
				By Interest	300	0	0
				By Law Changes	120	0	0
				By Stationery and Postages	100	0	0
				By Rent	200	0	0
				By Balance for Extras	58	15	0
	£15,050	0	0		£15,050	0	0

ESTIMATED REVENUE ACCOUNT

	£	s.	d.		£	s.	d.
To 400 Subscriptions of £5 5s	2,100	0	0	By Rent	200	0	0
				By Up-keep of Green	700	0	0
To Green Fees, Locker Rents, etc	100	0	0	By Professionals' Wages	40	0	0
				By Secretary's Salary	150	0	0
				By Fuel, Insurance, Rates and Taxes	150	0	0
				By Stationery, Postage etc.	75	0	0
				By First Mortgage Interest	160	0	0
				By Founders' Debenture Interest	400	0	0
				By First Mortgage Sinking Fund	130	0	0
				By Repairs, Prizes, etc.	195	0	0
	£2,200	0	0		£2,200	0	0

Appendix 3

SUNNINGDALE GOLF CLUB

RIDGE MOUNT,
SUNNINGDALE
JUNE 24TH, 1901

Dear Sir,

At a meeting held at the Café Monico, on April 29th, a resolution was passed by a large majority authorising the Committee to raise the sum of £4,000, necessary for the completion of the Course and Club House, in any way they might think advisable.

As, however, there seemed to be some doubt whether it would be legal to place this loan in front of the amount contributed by the original Founders without their unanimous consent, it has been thought desirable to have Counsel's opinion on the matter.

The Committee are advised by Messrs. A.R. Kirby and E.W. Martelli that there is nothing in the original agreement giving the Founders any specific charge upon any of the assets of the Club, and that, therefore, the Committee have full power (under the rules of the Club) to raise the amount necessary, in any way, on being requested to do so by a majority of the members.

At the Meeting referred to, a great many present stated that they should prefer advancing another £40 each, to having a mortgage on the Club House from an outside source, and the Committee, after a good deal of consideration, have adopted this course.

They therefore propose to issue 100 First Mortgage Debenture Bonds of £50 each, bearing interest at 4 per cent, of which it is proposed to call at present only £40-£20 on July 20th, and £20 on September 20th - to be secured upon the Club House, and paid off before the original amount contributed by the Founders, and to offer these in the first instance to the Founders, and afterwards, if necessary, to the other members of the Club.

The money to be raised by this means will in part be devoted to pay off about £3,000 which will become due to the Builders on the completion of the Club House. The balance will be used to pay for the necessary supply of water to the greens, and the cost of erecting the professional's workshop and caddies' house.

The form of Debenture Bond and Trust Deed, and an extract from the Building Contract, so as it affects the Contractors' charges, may be seen at the office of Messrs. Bircham & Co., 46 Parliament Street, S.W.

Now that the Club has a practically full membership there is very little doubt of being able during the next 20 years, by means of a Sinking Fund, to extinguish the First Mortgage Debentures, and to pay off sufficient of the existing Founders' Bonds to leave the balance amply secured by the lease of the Club House alone at dwelling house value.

As it is possible that some of the Founders may not feel disposed to take a Debenture, it will materially assist the Committee if those who are willing to take more than one would kindly do so in order that the necessary amount may be raised.

The Committee will be obliged by the enclosed Form being filled up and returned in the envelope sent herewith, by July 1st.

Yours faithfully,

M. ERSKINE
Secretary

Appendix 4

SUNNINGDALE GOLF CLUB

AUGUST 26TH, 1901

Dear Sir,

We have the pleasure to inform you that the Course will be opened for play on Monday, 23rd September, when the Club House will be ready for the use of Members. The official opening will be postponed to the Spring Meeting, 1902.

Mr. H.S. Colt has been elected Secretary, and Mr. J. White (late of Seaford), Professional, and Mr. and Mrs. A.W. Patterson (late of the Chislehurst Golf Club), have been appointed Steward and Stewardess. They commence their duties, September 16th.

The Committee will feel obliged by your forwarding the Entrance Fee due from you, viz., £   , accompanied by the pink Form sent herewith, to Messrs. Barclay & Co., Ltd., The Bank, Windsor, in the envelope enclosed for that purpose who will return you the receipt.

The £2 2s. you have already paid will cover your subscription to 31st December, 1901 ; the subscription, £5, 5s., for 1902, becoming due 1st January next.

Lockers are now being fixed, should you wish to have one allocated to you, the Committee will feel obliged by your filling up the green Form sent herewith and returning it in the envelope provided for that purpose.

With a view to the formation of a list of Handicaps, the Committee will be glad if you will also fill up and return the Handicap Form (yellow), accompanying this circular.

W.G. Rigden,
T.A. Roberts,
ON BEHALF OF THE COMMITTEE
OF THE SUNNINGDALE GOLF CLUB

161

Appendix 5

Sunningdale Golf Club

Lady visitors may be introduced by members for the purpose of playing on any day (except Saturdays, Sundays, Competition Days, Bank Holidays, or other Public Holidays, including the 1st days of May and November), on the same terms as may from time to time be in force respecting the admission of temporary Members. On Sundays Ladies may play in mixed foursomes after 3.15 p.m. Such Lady visitors shall in all cases play with the Member who introduces them. A match in which a lady is playing must allow an ordinary two-ball match to pass. No Ladies are permitted to play under any other conditions. Luncheons are not served to lady visitors, and no lady is allowed inside the Club House until after 4 p.m.

Appendix 6

Sunningdale Golf Club

BYE-LAWS made by the Committee to take effect from the 1st day of January, 1905.

GUESTS:-

A Member shall be entitled to introduce a guest to the Club House and Green on the following terms:-

To the Club House only, without payment.

To the Club House and Green on payment of the following fees:-

Three shillings per day on Saturday, Sunday, Competition day, Bank Holiday or Public Holiday, including the first of May and November. Two shillings per day on all other days.

In all cases the guest shall play with the Member introducing him. The Member is responsible for all payments in connection with the visit. No payment of any description shall be made by the guest with the exception of the above fees.

No guest can be introduced under this Bye-law on more than six days during the Club's financial year.

Members shall be entitled to introduce Ladies to Tea after 4 p.m. in the dining room of the Club House.

TEMPORARY MEMBERS:-

Visitors having a written introduction from a Member and after giving 48 hours notice may be admitted as Temporary Members of the Club on the following terms:-

Ten shillings per day on Saturday, Sunday, Competition day, Bank Holiday or Public Holiday, including the first days of May and November.

Five shillings per day on all other days.

Twenty shillings for one week.

In all cases their admission shall be subject to the approval of the Committee. If the Committee refuse to admit a person under this Bye-law, such person shall not be eligible as a guest under the preceding Bye-law.

Appendix 7

Sunningdale Golf Club
Spirits

	COST PRICE		SALE PRICE	
	Per Gls.	Per Bot.	Per Gls.	Per Bot.
SCOTCH WHISKY	4d	3/4	8d	6/8
SCOTCH WHISKY S.G.C.	4¹/₅d	3/6	8d	6/8
IRISH WHISKY	4d	3/4	8d	6/8
BRANDY	5d	4/2	8d	6/8
GIN	3d	2/6	6d	5/-
RUM	3³/₅d	3/-	6d	5/-
I. JAMESON	5d	4/-	8d	6/8

Wines

	COST PRICE		SALE PRICE	
	Per Gls.	Per Bot.	Per Gls.	Per Bot.
SHERRY, PALE	3¹/₅d	2/8	6d	5/-
SHERRY O. BROWN	4d	3/3	6d	5/-
PORT -				
1896 Vin. Bottles	6¹/₂d	4/4	9d	6/-
1896 Vin. Pints		2/2		3/6
BEST O.T.	5¹/₅d	3/6	9d	6/-
2nd O.T	4¹/₂d	3/-	6d	4/-
O.T Pints		1/9		3/6
WHITE	4¹/₁₀d	2/9	6d	4/-
CLARET -				
Claret Bottles		1/3		2/-
Claret Pints		9d		1/3
MARSALA				6d
MOSELLE-				
Moselle Bottles		2/11		4/-
Moselle Pints		1/7		2/6
LAUBENHEIM		1/5¹/₂		2/3
Laubenheim		10d		1/3
BURGUNDY		1/6		2/-
ZELTINGER Bottles		1/8		2/3
ZELTINGER Pints		11d		1/3
HOCK				
Hock Bottles		2/-		3/6
Hock Pints		1/-		2/-
CHAMPAGNES -				
DEUTZ & GELDERMAN, Bottles		6/3		10/-
DEUTZ & GELDERMAN, Pints		4/-		5/6
POMEROY & GRENO, Bottles		8/10¹/₂		12/-
POMEROY & GRENO, Pints		3/3		5/6
LEMOINE MAGNUMS		15/6		21/-
LEMOINE MAGNUMS, Bottles		7/10		12/-
LEMOINE MAGNUMS, Pints		4/2		6/6
ROEDERER, Bottles		7/6		10/6
ROEDERER, Pints		3/11		5/6

Beers

	COST PRICE		SALE PRICE	
	Per Gls.	Per Bot.	Per Gls.	Per Bot.
LAGER, Large		4¹/₂d		6d
LAGER, Small		3d		4d
L. DARK LAGER		3¹/₂d		6d
S. DARK LAGER		2¹/₂d		4d
BASS, Large		4¹/₂d		6d
BASS, Small		2¹/₂d		4d
STOUT, Large		4d		6d
STOUT, Small		2¹/₂d		4d
STOUT, Russian, Large		7¹/₂d		1/-
STOUT, Russian, Small		5d		6d
CIDER, Bottles		3¹/₂d		6d
ALE, Draught		1/6 gal	2d	2/8 gal
CIDER, Draught		1/8 gal	2d	2/8 gal
STOUT, Draught			2d	
ALE, Staff		1/- gal		
RUSSIAN BEER		5d		8d
5X		6d		9d

Aerated Waters

	COST PRICE		SALE PRICE	
	Per Gls.	Per Bot.	Per Gls.	Per Bot.
APPOLLINARIS, Large		4d		4d
APPOLLINARIS, Small		3d		2d
SODA WATER, Large		1d		4d
SODA WATER, Small		³/₄d		2d
SELTZER, Large		1d		4d
SELTZER, Small		³/₄d		2d
GINGER BEER		1d		3d
LEMONADE		1d		3d
SCHWEPPE'S SODA WATER, Large		2¹/₂d		6d
SCHWEPPE'S SODA WATER, Small		1¹/₂d		3d
SALUTARIS, Large		2d		6d
SALUTARIS, Small		1¹/₂d		3d
GINGER ALE, Large		2¹/₂d		4d
GINGER ALE, Small		1¹/₂d		2d
PERRIER, Large		4d		4d
PERRIER, Small		3d		2d

Liqueurs

	COST PRICE		SALE PRICE	
	Per Gls.	Per Bot.	Per Gls.	Per Bot.
CURACOA	2²/₃d	6/-	4d	9/8
KUMMEL	2¹/₅d	4/3	4d	7/8
CHARTREUSE, YELLOW	2²/₃d	8/6	6d	19/6
CHARTREUSE, GREEN	3¹/₂d	10/6	6d	19/6
MARASCHINO	3d	5/6	4d	7/4
CHERRY BRANDY	1¹/₂d	4/-	4d	11/4
GINGER BRANDY	4²/₅d	3/6	6d	5/-
LIQUEUR BRANDY, Best	5¹/₂d	12/6	9d	20/3
LIQUEUR BRANDY, 2nd	3¹/₉d	7/-	6d	13/6
VERMOUTH	2¹/₂d	2/6	6d	6/-
BENEDICTINE	2¹/₂d	7/6	4d	12/4
SLOE GIN	3d	3/4	4d	4/8
CREME de MENTHE	2d	5/-	4d	9/8
LIME JUICE	1d	1/-	4d	3/4
X. O.	5¹/₂d	11/8	9d	20/3
V. O.	3d	6/3	6d	13/6
CHERRY WHISKEY	3¹/₂d	4/4	6d	9/-
DAMSON GIN	2d	2/6		4/-

Cigars

	COST PRICE		SALE PRICE	
	Per Cig.	Per 100	Per Cig.	Per 100
J.S.M., IMPERIALES	9d	75/-	1/-	100/-
J.S.M., CELESTIALES	7¹/₅d	60/-	9d	75/-
UPMANN	4¹/₃d	36/-	6d	50/-
VILLA Y VILLAS	3d	25/-	4d	33/4
CIGARETTES				
TURKISH		7/3	1d	8/4
EGYPTIAN FREEMAN		6/6	1d	8/4
VIRGINIAN	¹/₂d		¹/₂d	
TOBACCOS				
J.A. & N.S. MIXTURE	4¹/₂d oz	6/4 oz	6d oz	8/- oz
PLAYER'S NAVY CUT	4¹/₂d oz	6/- oz	5d oz	6/8 oz
SMITH'S YELLOW	4¹/₂d oz	6/- oz	5d oz	6/8 oz
PIPES	10d		1/-	
FUSEES	³/₄d		1d	
STOCKINGS	4/6		6/-	
SOCKS	1/-		2/-	

Appendix 8

SUNNINGDALE GOLF CLUB

MAY 4TH, 1909

Dear Sir,

During the past winter, Evening Continuation Classes have been held for the Caddies, under the Education Committee of the Surrey County Council. A first rate teacher, Mr. Munro, from the Bagshot Schools was appointed, and the Committee have been most pleased with the results.

As no other room was available to meet the requirements of the Council, the Classes were held in the Committee Room, and several members of the Club kindly consented to act with the Committee as Managers.

The Committee desire to thank those Members for their assistance. Between 40 and 50 boys attended the Classes, and a copy of Mr. Munro's report is printed overleaf.

In addition to these Classes, Club making was taught by a competent Club maker, in the workshop adjoining the Caddies' Room, and the results in this respect have been also satisfactory.

Now that the work has passed the experimental stage, it is desired to place it upon a permanent footing, and the Committee feel sure that the Members realise the responsibility of the Club, and will wish it to take a prominent part in the movement for the improvement of the position of Caddies. It is generally admitted that, unless care be taken, the occupation of carrying is likely to lead to the creation of an unemployable class, and the present movement here has been taken with a view to the prevention of this. Boys over the age of 17 are not now registered as Caddies, and an effort is being made to place the regular Caddies over that age in permanent employment.

The success up to the present seems to justify an expenditure upon a building of a more permanent structure than the present wooden shed, and it is desired to establish a fund amounting to about £1,000, to defray the cost of such a building, which will provide a class room and a recreation and refreshment room for Caddies. This class room will be used for the Evening Continuation Classes under the County Council, and the existing wooden building will be used for technical classes for Club making and Carpentering, and other like subjects. The boys are instructed in matters having a direct bearing upon their lives.

Towards this sum a most generous donation has been made by a member of the Club of the sum of £250, and it is thought that there should not be any great difficulty in obtaining the balance by donations from those interested in the work. A suitable building could be erected at a cost of from £600 to £800, and the balance would be used for the proper equipment of the rooms, and anything over would be invested to produce an income, to bear the annual cost of carrying on the Classes.

This Club has up to the present taken a prominent part in the movement, and many applications are now received from other Clubs, desiring to have particulars of what is being done in this way at Sunningdale.

Donations can be sent to the Secretary.

I am, dear Sir,
Your obedient Servant,
H.S. COLT,
Secretary

Sunningdale Golf Club

CADDIES

Arrangements have now been made whereby all the Caddies will be engaged under a fixed contract with the Club, at a fixed wage with fixed hours of attendance, and with definite duties in addition to the carrying of Golf clubs.

The boys will be divided into three classes in future, the charges for which will be as follows:-

1st Class	*1/6 per round*
2nd Class	*1/4 per round*
3rd Class	*1/3 per round*

This tariff will come into force on Monday, Nov. 15th, 1909.

NO LUNCHEON MONEY will be paid, and the booking fees will be abolished. All the Caddies in the future will be able to obtain from the Caddie Master an advance in respect of their weekly wages up to a certain amount, so that they may be able to obtain lunch if they have not brought it with them, nor sufficient money to pay for it.

Up to the present time, it has been no doubt the custom amongst members who play one round in the morning to pay the Caddie his luncheon money, and this with the fee for the round and the booking fee has come to a total of 1/7 for the one round. Many members in the past, who have only played a round in the afternoon, have no doubt given the Caddie something for his tea, and now that this will be abolished in addition to luncheon money, the Committee thinks that the proposed arrangements will not prove any more expensive than the tariff up to the present.

It is submitted that the scheme whereby the caddies will be engaged under a fixed contract and thus become servants of the Club, will be of great advantage to the boys, and will put a stop to the loafing habits which are usually associated with carrying.

The Committee desire to thank the members for their generous response to the subsciption list for building a new Caddie House, which ought to be ready for use in about a fortnight's time. Some of the evening classes are at present conducted in the Committee Room and others in the Carpenter's Shop, and have been well attended.

H.S. COLT

November 1st, 1909   *Secretary*

Appendix 9

Sunningdale Golf Club

BERKS

JUNE 14TH, 1911

The Committee have been approached by some of the residents in the neighbourhood to ascertain if the Club would be willing to let a portion of the land now held on lease and not used, and if so upon what terms, so that such land might be included in a new nine-hole course to be made by a separate Club.

As stated in the last Annual Report, which was adopted by the Club in January, it is generally thought better that the additional nine-hole course which it is now proposed to make, should be made by a separate organisation, the interests of the Club being safeguarded by a condition that members of your Club be enabled to join on favourable terms.

The additional facilities for Golf thereby provided would thus be gained without enlarging the membership of your Club to provide the funds for extra Club house accommodation, cost of constructing the Links, and the necessary revenue which would be required for the formation and upkeep of the course.

It is generally considered desirable that the scenery which surrounds the Links should not be destroyed by the erection of a multitude of houses. This object to a large extent would be obtained by the adoption of the scheme which is now proposed, for the buildings which would be built would be limited to a few houses, and those would be at a considerable distance from the Links, namely, on the crest of the Hill which lies on the East side of the 18th Hole.

The Committee, after full consideration, make the following recommendations:-

That a lease should be granted of the land coloured pink on the enclosed plan on the following terms:-

(1) Rent: £2 per acre

(2) Full Members and Provisional Members of the S.G.C. to be eligible as Members of the new Club, always without entrance fee, on paying a subscription of £2 2s 0d per annum, the other Members to pay £3 3s 0d at least.

(3) The S.G.C. Members to be allowed to introduce Ladies as Visitors on payment of a Green fee of 2/6 per diem on any day of the week.

The proposed new Course has been carefully surveyed, and it is considered that the ground is capable of being made into nine good holes; it will be observed that these will in no way interfere with the present Course.

Before binding the Club in any way in this matter the Committee desire to take a vote of the Members, and as it will be difficult to obtain a representative meeting at this time of the year, they have decided to take a referendum, and if the result be favourable they will sanction the scheme on the above lines, the further details to be settled by them in the best interests of the Club.

Kindly sign the enclosed post card, and if opposed to the scheme insert the word "not" between the words "am" and "in", and return it before the 24th instant, when the votes will be counted.

By order of the Committee
H.S. COLT
K. GREENWAY
Joint Secretaries

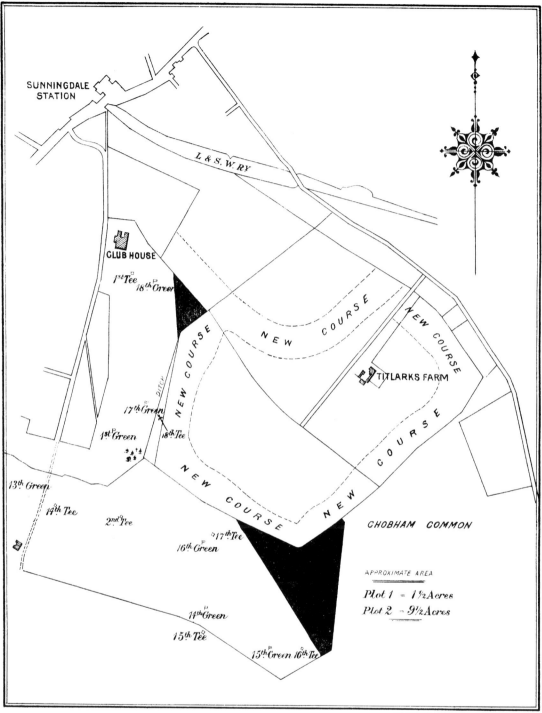

SUNNINGDALE STATION

L & S. W. RY

CLUB HOUSE

1st Tee
18th Green

NEW COURSE

NEW COURSE

NEW COURSE

TITLARKS FARM

17th Green

1st Green

18th Tee

DITCH

13th Green

14th Tee

2nd Tee

17th Tee

16th Green

NEW COURSE

NEW COURSE

CHOBHAM COMMON

14th Green

15th Tee

15th Green 16th Tee

APPROXIMATE AREA

Plot 1 = 1½ Acres
Plot 2 = 9½ Acres

BRADLEY & SON, LTD., READING

172

Appendix 10

SUNNINGDALE HEATH GOLF CLUB

AUGUST 6TH, 1919

To the Debenture-holders

Sunningdale <u>Heath</u> Golf Club

As you are probably aware the maintenance of the Club during the past years has only been made possible by the consideration of the Lessors in waiving the payment of all rent, by liberal contributions on the part of the neighbouring residents, and by no payment of interest on the Debentures. For a long time past, when it became evident that the Club had no immediate prospect of expansion and that even its existence was extremely precarious, it was hoped that sooner or later the course might be taken over by the Sunningdale Golf Club, as an alternative course. This, subject to the approval of the members of the Sunningdale Club and the Debenture-holders of this Club, can now be done. We have to accept the fact that under existing circumstances the Debentures have very little, if any, realisable value. On the other hand the Committee of the Sunningdale Club recognise there is a considerable amount of substantial value in the course as it stands for the purposes which they contemplate, and they have made an offer, subject to the approval of their members for which purpose a meeting has been convened, to purchase the whole of the Debentures of the Heath Club for £875, or 25% of their face value. This offer the Trustees have provisionally accepted subject to ratification by the Debenture-holders, and they strongly recommend its acceptance in view of the constant risk of the total failure of the Club, in which case the Debenture-holders would get nothing at all. Under this arrangement the course will be maintained and improved by the elimination of the seventh and eighth holes, and the Sunningdale Heath Club wll be wound up.

If you wish to support the above arrangement kindly sign and return the enclosed form.

F.A. GOVETT
T.A. ROBERTS
Trustees

SUNNINGDALE HEATH GOLF CLUB

SEPTEMBER 1ST, 1919

Dear Sir or Madam

Subjoined is a copy of a Circular which recently was sent to the Debenture Holders of this Club. At the Meeting of the Sunningdale Golf Club to which reference is made therein, the proposal of the Committee of that Club to purchase the Lease held by the Heath Club was approved and adopted, and since then the offer to purchase has been accepted by the Debenture Holders of this Club.

I have in consequence to inform you that this Club will cease to exist as from September 30th, when the Course will be taken over by Sunningdale Golf Club.

Regulations as to Conditions under which players who are not members of that Club may use the Links will no doubt be drawn up in due course.

As a result of this all future liability for Annual Subscriptions will now cease, except on the part of a few members who are in arrear with their subscriptions for the current year, and those who have been good enough to guarantee the deficit for the current year. Members who have given orders to their Bankers to pay the subscription falling due on October 1st are requested to cancel the same.

By order of the Committee
Yours faithfully
E.E. VILLIERS,
Hon. Sec.

Appendix 11

𝔖𝔲𝔫𝔫𝔦𝔫𝔤𝔡𝔞𝔩𝔢 𝔊𝔬𝔩𝔣 ℭ𝔩𝔲𝔟

DECEMBER, 1949

Dear Sir,

Following on Mr. d'Abo's circular letter to you, the following gentlemen have consented to serve with me on a Caretaker Committee to carry on the affairs of the Club till the Annual General Meeting, when the Captain and a full Committee can be constitutionally elected:-

F.S.A. Baker	E.B. McInerney
T.V. Boardman	G.A. Roberts
P.B. Lucas	S.G. Sillem

The closing of the accounts will be expedited so that the Annual Meeting can be held as early as possible in the New Year.

It is imperative to take immediate steps to remedy the unfortunate position in which the Club finds itself today. In view of the approaching end of our financial year, time does not permit of Members being consulted and this Committee has therefore taken the following decisions:

(1) <u>Subscriptions.</u> This Committee has decided by virtue of the powers given it by Rule VIII not to implement the Resolution of the Extraordinary General Meeting to increase Subscriptions, but in order to assist the Club in the meantime, this Committee has decided to invite Members, particularly those paying the lower rates of Subscription of ten and twelve guineas per annum, as a temporary measure to make some voluntary addition to their Subscriptions, having regard to the amount they use the Club and it is hoped that all regular playing Members will respond generously to this invitation. This extra revenue is urgently required to help make good next year's anticipated Deficit of £1,500, and it is hoped that as many Members as possible will contribute.

(2) <u>Lady Members.</u> It was resolved at the General Meeting that this matter should be postponed for a year. This Committee intends to place it on the Agenda for discussion at the Annual Meeting when it will be possible to form an approximate idea of the Club's income for the year, having regard to the appeal for extra subscriptions and to the issue of Bonds. In the meantime this Committee will explore the possibilities and cost of providing suitable amenities for Ladies on the Club premises.

(3) <u>Bonds.</u> It was also resolved at the Extraordinary General Meeting to issue Bonds in units of £25 to Members, each unit to carry with it a reduction of 10/6d in the Member's subscription.

Full particulars and application forms will be sent out as soon as possible.

(4) <u>Annual General Meeting.</u> In addition to the ordinary business, this Committee desires to give Members every opportunity for a full and frank discussion of any matter relating to the constitution of the Club and the management of its affairs.

Due notice of any subject for discussion must be submitted in writing to the Secretary not later than 15th January, 1950.

As regards the election of the Captain and Committee, nominations will be received up to 15th January 1950. Candidiates must be duly proposed and seconded, and their previous assent to serve must have been obtained. It is not proposed to confine the voting to those actually present at the Meeting and voting papers will be sent to all Members. These must be returned not later than one week before the date of the Meeting.

This Committee of course appreciates that it is acting in a somewhat arbitrary and unconstitutional manner but existing circumstances preclude the possibility of doing otherwise. It is not anticipated that other matters will arise during this Committee's period of office, which will call for action contrary to the Rules of the Club.

Finally, and with the full concurrence of this Committee, I should like to stress that it would be, to say the least of it, tragic were this Club by reason of dissension to forfeit its unrivalled position in the world of Golf. I must therefore earnestly appeal to all Members to sink their differences and to pull together especially at this time.

Yours sincerely
T.E. CUNNINGHAM

Appendix 12

𝔖𝔲𝔫𝔫𝔦𝔫𝔤𝔡𝔞𝔩𝔢 𝔊𝔬𝔩𝔣 ℭ𝔩𝔲𝔟

MARCH 23RD, 1950

Dear Sir,

At the Annual General Meeting held on Sunday, 26th February 1950, the following result of the ballot for Captain and Committee was announced:-

Captain: T.E. Cunningham

Committee:

T.V. Boardman	Brig. Gen. A.C. Critchley
P.B. Lucas	A.A. McNair
S.G. Sillem	C.G. Donaldson
R.J. Breyfogle	E.B. McInerney
N.C. Selway	

After the formal business of the Meeting had been concluded, the Captain explained that the newly elected Committee had clearly not yet had time to consider the many problems that confronted the Club, and were therefore, not in a position to place any concrete proposals before the Meeting.

Accordingly the following resolution was proposed, seconded and carried unanimously.

"That this General Meeting approves of the issue by the Committee to all Members of a Circular, expressing their views, and a Questionnaire relating to the admission of Lady Members and the Finance and General Direction of the Club, and authorises the Committee to take whatever action they consider appropriate, giving effect as far as possible to the wishes of the Majority of Members, as expressed in their replies."

Since the Annual General Meeting the Committee have met and report to the Members as follows:-

Having examined the financial and general position of the Club, the Committee are of the unanimous opinion that, having regards to the Club's commitments in the form of two courses and a large Clubhouse, it is not under present conditions, a feasible proposition to run the Club on the present membership without raising subscriptions.

The Committee are reluctant to recommend an increase in the rates of subscription. At the same time they feel that their primary duty to the Members is to ensure that the Club's finances are put on to a sound basis and it must be recognised that, if their efforts to increase the income of the Club by other means do not prove successful, they may have no option but to raise the subscription next year.

The Committee feel, therefore, that their initial efforts should be directed towards attracting more members at the present level of subscriptions.

It is felt that the Club's failure to attract members in adequate numbers since the War has been due to a lack of realisation of the present-day requirements and expectations of golfers both inside and outside the Clubhouse. In particular, it is thought that Members have been lost through our failure to give to Ladies the same facilities that they enjoy at so many other Clubs, particularly in our own immediate neighbourhood, with the result that married golfers - particularly the younger ones - who might have joined Sunningdale, have gone elsewhere.

The Committee, therefore, unanimously recommend to Members that Ladies be eligible for Associate Membership of the Club.

Please indicate your general agreement or otherwise by writing "Yes" or "No".

If you have any modification or suggestions to make, please state them briefly below:-

Signed ....

I enclose cheque £   s.   d. as voluntary contribution to the Club's Funds.

Signed ....

𝔖𝔲𝔫𝔫𝔦𝔫𝔤𝔟𝔞𝔩𝔢 𝔊𝔬𝔩𝔣 ℭ𝔩𝔲𝔟

Are you in favour of the election to the Club of Associate Lady Members on the following terms:-

1. <u>Election.</u>
   To be proposed and seconded by two Men Members and to be elected by the Committee.

2. <u>Voting Rights.</u>
   Associate Lady Members will have no voting rights and will not be entitled to attend General Meetings.

3. <u>Playing Rights.</u>
   <u>Mondays to Fridays inclusive</u>
   Equal rights with men on both courses.
   <u>Saturdays, Sundays, Bank Holidays and Competition Days</u>

<u>Old Course</u>   To start only between 11 a.m. and 1 p.m. or after 3 p.m. until the New Course is in full operation when the matter will be reviewed.

<u>New Course</u>   Unrestricted rights of play.

4. <u>Guests.</u>
   Ladies will be entitled to introduce guests on the same terms as Men.

5. <u>Subscriptions.</u> (on the basis of a 14 guinea subscription for men)
   Full Member and Wife: 21 guineas
   Other lady members of family: 7 guineas
   Junior Member and Wife: 12 guineas
   Single Ladies: 10 guineas
   Non-playing Members: 3 guineas

6. <u>Accommodation.</u>
   The Committee have carefully considered what improved accommodation can be provided for Ladies and have decided to proceed with the first part of the plan which has been exhibited in the Club for the past few weeks.

Appendix 13

Sunningdale Golf Club
BERKS

DECEMBER, 1947

Dear Sir,

ADMISSION OF LADY GUESTS OF MEMBERS TO THE
READING ROOM AND DINING ROOM

As the Referendum on this Subject resulted in a large majority in favour of both proposals, the Committee has decided that both rooms shall be opened forthwith to Lady Guests accompanied by Members.

The Ladies' Entrance will be by the Verandah Door Facing the practice putting green.

A Member may only bring two Ladies to lunch at any one time and the Steward must be notified by Wednesday for the following week-end.

A charge of 2/6 Table Money will be made for any Lady for whom a Green Fee has not been paid.

It is regretted that the conversion of the old war-time Club Room Annexe to a Ladies' Cloak Room has not been completed, but this will be made available as soon as possible.

G.G. KIRKE,
Secretary

180

Captains.

1901	H.H.LONGMAN.
1902	H.H.LONGMAN.
1903	The EARL of ELDON.
1904	HENLEY CARLOS CLARKE.
1905	The LORD STANLEY.
1906	WILLIAM TROTTER.
1907	W.G.RIGDEN.
1908	Sir EDGAR VINCENT, *K.C.M.G.*
1909	C.M.WOODBRIDGE.
1910	H.H.PRINCE ALBERT of Schleswig Holstein.
1911	T.A.ROBERTS.
1912	H.A.TROTTER.
1913	P.J. de PARAVICINI.
1914	N.F.HUNTER.
1915	N.F.HUNTER.
1916	N.F.HUNTER.
1919	F HEYWOOD.
1920	ANGUS V.HAMBRO, *M.P.*
1921	LORD DUNEDIN, *P.C.,K.C.V.O.*
1922	LORD DUNEDIN, *P.C.,K.C.V.O.*
1923	LORD DUNEDIN, *P.C.,G.C.V.O.*
1924	H.S.COLT.
1925	Sir GORDON CAMPBELL, *K.B.E.*
1926	VISCOUNT DUNEDIN, *P.C.,G.C.V.O.*
1927	J.M.OLDHAM.
1927	T.A.ROBERTS.
1928	C.J.BURNUP.
1929	A.H.READ.
1930	H.R.H.The PRINCE of WALES, *K.G.*
1931	Sir JOSEPH SKEVINGTON, *K.C.V.O.,F.R.C.S.*
1932	H.R.H.The DUKE of YORK, *K.G.*
1933	J.S.F.MORRISON, *D.F.C.*
1934	A.T.TURQUAND-YOUNG.
1935	R.H.ANKETELL.
1936	D.H.KYLE.
1937	Sir ROBERT McLEAN.
1938	Sir FERGUS MORTON.
1939	W.E.BAYLEY.
1940	G.D.FOX, *M.C.*
1946	JAMES MOIR.
1947	JAMES MOIR.
1948	T.E.CUNNINGHAM.
1949	G.L.d'ABO.
1950	T.E.CUNNINGHAM.
1951	C.G.DONALDSON.
1952	A.A.McNAIR.
1953	J.B.P.WILLIAMSON.
1954	Sir FREDERICK BAKER.
1955	G.E.BEHARRELL.
1956	J.D.A.LANGLEY.
1957	A.C.SNOWDEN.
1958	R.J.BREYFOGLE.
1959	VERNON G.SMITH.
1960	G.H.MICKLEM.
1961	JAMES WILSON.

Captains.

1962	P. J. P. DONALD.
1963	Captain F. B. LLOYD, *O.B.E., R.N.*
1964	L. W NEEDHAM, *M.C.*
1965	E. P. SHAW.
1966	J. K. PEPPERCORN.
1967	J. C. WOLFF, *M.B.E.*
1968	G. R. ROUGIER. *C.B.E., Q.C.*
1969	Sir KENNETH HAGUE.
1970	P. S. CLARK.
1971	JOHN WHITFIELD, *J.P.*
1972	JOSEPH DEEKS, *M.B.E.*
1973	NICHOLAS ROYDS.
1974	T. U. HARTWRIGHT
1975	Major-General P. R. LEUCHARS, *C.B.E.*
1976	J. R. BOARDMAN.
1977	T. E. D. HARKER.
1978	G. S. STONE.
1979	D. H. R. HOLLAND.
1980	JEFFREY AGATE.
1981	A. HANBURY.
1982	C. R. BURN.
1983	G. B. YOUNG.
1984	V. M. SHAW.
1985	J. K. TULLIS.
1986	D. A. O. DAVIES.
1987	J. C. MATHEW, *Q.C.*
1988	R. H. THOMPSON.
1989	J. M. C. PUCKRIDGE
1990	K. C. KNOCKER
1991	RICHARD L. M. MORRIS
1992	MICHAEL HUGHESDON
1993	D. S. YOUNG
1994	H. U. S. McMICHEN
1995	R. J. G. SHAW
1996	B. G. STREATHER
1997	ANTHONY BIGGINS
1998	C. J. B. NEEDHAM
1999	C. P. C. DONALD

The Captain, Vice-Captain and Past Captains attending their annual dinner with the members of the Committee on 26th February, 1999.
Seated (from left) N.C. Royds, J.C. Wolff, C.J.B. Needham, P.J.P. Donald, C.P.C. Donald, J.F. Whitfield and Maj. Gen: P.R. Leuchars.
Standing (from left) J.R. Boardman, R.H. Thompson, D.H.R. Holland, J.C. Mathew QC, G.J. Agate, J.M.C. Puckridge, A. Hanbury, M.C. Hughesdon, C.R. Burn, Dr. H.U.S. McMichen, J.K. Tullis, D.S. Young, B.G. Streather and D.A.O. Davies.

Club Gold Medal (Scratch)

SPRING

1902	M.W. MOSSOP	83
1903	A.C.M. CROOME	85
1904	H.G.B. ELLIS	84
1905	H.E. HAMBRO	79
1906	C.C. LINGEN	76
1907	G.C. CAMPBELL	76
1908	W.P. TINDAL-ATKINSON	76
1909	H.E. TAYLOR	75
1910	H.E. TAYLOR	74
1911	H.E. TAYLOR	78
1912	H.E. TAYLOR	73
1913	H.E. TAYLOR	78
1914	A.H. READ	76
1919	J. MURRAY-WOODS	80
1920	Major G.C. CAMPBELL	77
1921	D. GRANT	75
1922	Col. H.E. HAMBRO	76
1923	E.R. CAMPBELL	74
1924	Capt. R.H. JOBSON M.C.	73
1925	Capt. S.K. THORBURN M.C.	74
1926	Capt. R.H. JOBSON M.C.	74
1927	E.R. CAMPBELL	74
1928	Capt. R.H. JOBSON M.C.	78
1929	Major S.K. THORBURN M.C.	78
1930	R.W. HARTLEY	72
1931	D.H. KYLE	75
1932	R.W. HARTLEY	70
1933	Major S.K. THORBURN M.C.	72
1934	D.H. KYLE	71
1935	R.W. HARTLEY	75
1936	I.M. WATERS	73
1937	L.G. CRAWLEY	70
1938	L.G. CRAWLEY	70
1939	E.F. STOREY	72
1947	L.G. CRAWLEY	73
1948	ROBERT SWEENY	72
1949	J.O.H. GREENLY	74
1950	L.G. CRAWLEY	71
1951	G.H. MICKLEM	73
1952	J.D.A. LANGLEY	72
1953	J.D.A. LANGLEY	73
1954	V.G. SMITH	74
1955	R.W. KREFTING	72
1956	D.W. FRAME	72
1957	D.W. FRAME	69
1958	G.H. FOSTER	71
1959	D.W. FRAME	75
1960	D.W. FRAME	71
1961	M.D. DAWSON	72
1962	I. CALDWELL	71
1963	B. CRITCHLEY	73
1964	I. CALDWELL	70

Club Gold Medal (Scratch)

SPRING

Year	Name	Score
1965	R.HUNTER	74
1966	I.CALDWELL	71
1967	B.CRITCHLEY	73
1968	A.J.HOWARD	72
1969	E.R.DEXTER	73
1970	R.HUNTER	70
1971	R.HUNTER	70
1972	M.C.HUGHESDON	69
1973	J.L.McCLUE	74
1974	J.C.DAVIES	70
1975	M.C.HUGHESDON	75
1976	J.C.DAVIES	70
1977	J.K.TULLIS	78
1978	J.C.DAVIES	72
1979	A.R.KERR	72
1980	R.HUNTER	71
1981	A.R.KERR	70
1982	B.G.STREATHER	72
1983	R.HUNTER	73
1984	E.R.DEXTER	69
1985	M.C.HUGHESDON	71
1986	M.C.HUGHESDON	73
1987	E.R.DEXTER	75
1988	M.DEVETTA	69
1989	P.D.M.CARR	73
1990	M.DEVETTA	68
1991	J.H.R.KELLOCK	71
1992	H.C.A.ROWE	72
1993	M.C.HUGHESDON	71
1994	P.D.M.CARR	73
1995	T.J.C.JENKINS	71
1996	P.F.GARNER	75
1997	J.PUTT	74
1998	J.GALLACHER	72
1999	T.GOTTSTEIN	73

Club Gold Medal (Scratch)

Autumn

1902	The Hon. OSMUND SCOTT	80
1903	The Hon. DENYS SCOTT	82
1904	The Hon. OSMUND SCOTT	75
1905	J.S.WORTHINGTON	79
1906	G.C.CAMPBELL	78
1907	H.J.ROSS	80
1908	H.S.COLT	75
1909	N.F.HUNTER	74
1910	J.S.WORTHINGTON	75
1911	H.S.COLT	75
1912	H.E.TAYLOR	75
1913	Lord Charles HOPE	78
1919	Capt. The Hon. R.COKE	79
1920	R.H.de MONTMORENCY	78
1921	A.H.READ	76
1922	C.J.H.TOLLEY	75
1923	J.F.IRELAND M.C.	75
1924	Capt. S.K.THORBURN M.C.	72
1925	Capt. A.G.PEARSON D.S.O.	72
1926	H.GARDINER-HILL	73
1927	Major S.K.THORBURN M.C.	70
1928	D.E.LANDALE	69
1929	C.D.GRAY	74
1930	D.H.KYLE	71
1931	D.H.KYLE	74
1932	Capt C.G.B.STEVENS	73
1933	D.H.KYLE	73
1934	W.L.HARTLEY	73
1935	F.L.RANKIN	67
1936	T.E.CUNNINGHAM	71
1937	A.A.McNAIR	69
1938	L.G.CRAWLEY	71
1946	A.A.McNAIR	74
1947	L.G.CRAWLEY	69
1948	L.G.CRAWLEY	69
1949	S.M.McCREADY	70
1950	L.G.CRAWLEY	72
1951	P.F.McDONALD	68
1952	G.H.MICKLEM	70
1953	H.G.BENTLEY	72
1954	G.H.MICKLEM	72
1955	G.R.BRISTOWE	66
1956	G.B.WOLSTENHOLME	71
1957	G.T.DUNCAN	68
1958	D.W.FRAME	72
1959	M.D.DAWSON	73
1960	J.L.McCLUE	69
1961	J.L.McCLUE	72
1962	R.HUNTER	73
1963	B.CRITCHLEY	75
1964	J.L.McCLUE	71
1965	J.K.TULLIS	72

Club Gold Medal (Scratch)

Autumn

Year	Name	Score
1966	R.HUNTER	72
1967	R.HUNTER	68
1968	D.S.YOUNG	71
1969	R.SWEENY D.F.C.	73
1970	R.HUNTER	68
1971	J.L.McCLUE	69
1972	M.H.DIXON	68
1973	B.CRITCHLEY	72
1974	D.A.C.MARR	72
1975	B.CRITCHLEY	72
1976	A.G.BENZIE	73
1977	M.H.DIXON	72
1978	M.C.HUGHESDON	68
1979	J.C.DAVIES	72
1980	J.C.DAVIES	70
1981	I.CALDWELL	73
1982	J.C.DAVIES	72
1983	R.F.H.PETCH	76
1984	M.DEVETTA	74
1985	M.C.HUGHESDON	72
1986	A.J.HOWARD	69
1987	M.C.HUGHESDON	66
1988	J.H.R.KELLOCK	68
1989	J.H.R.KELLOCK	70
1990	M.H.DIXON	71
1991	C.B.MANSON	74
1992	M.C.HUGHESDON	70
1993	P.D.M.CARR	70
1994	D.J.G.ROYDS	71
1995	J.J.CARR	70
1996	P.D.M.CARR	72
1997	J.H.R.KELLOCK	72
1998	M.H.DIXON	73
1999	R.CALDWELL	70

Founders' Cup

SINGLES

1902	R.CREASY	Handicap	4
1903	A.C.M.CROOM		+1
1904	C.C.LINGEN		3
1905	E.W.WATERER		8
1906	F.G.WATERER		8
1907	A.TINDAL-ATKINSON		3
1908	Major H.De PRÉE		14
1909	E.A.SMIRKE		+2
1910	C.J.BURNUP		2
1911	A.J.HEALING		Scr.
1912	F.M.M.CARLISLE		Scr.
1913	J.M.OLDHAM		10
1914	A.TINDAL-ATKINSON		Scr.
1919	Capt. The Hon. R.COKE		3
1920	Major A.C.McLACHLAN		10
1921	J.R.A.STROYAN		4
1922	F.LAZENBY		8
1923	T.A.BOURN		2
1924	Sir FISHER DILK		6
1925	F.L.RANKIN		1
1926	Col. CHRISTIE C.M.G., D.S.O.		8
1927	J.MURRAY WOODS		Scr.
1928	L.F.LAZENBY		12
1929	P.LINDLEY		14
1930	F.B.BURTON		10
1931	Brig. Gen. A.C.CRITCHLEY C.M.G., D.S.O.		Scr.
1932	Sir ROBERT McLEAN		1
1933	C.SWEENY		Scr.
1934	N.C.SELWAY		1
1935	L.M.CLARK		5
1936	J.van ZWANENBERG		2
1937	F.C.O.VALENTINE		9
1938	W.J.B.GIRARDET		3
1939	R.BYASS		8
1947	R.Le CRON		6
1948	The EARL of LINDSAY		12
1949	Major H.RUSSELL		6
1950	V.G.SMITH		1
1951	A.ABELES		5
1952	T.U.HARTWRIGHT		11
1953	T.U.HARTWRIGHT		8
1954	Major W.D.HENDERSON		1
1955	P.W.G.NEEDHAM		2
1956	T.U.HARTWRIGHT		5
1957	A.ABELES		5
1958	J.D.I.COWPER		5
1959	Col. N.IRELAND-SMITH		6
1960	S.K.MAXWELL		11
1961	A.N.BEACH		8
1962	R.D.A.GALBRAITH		4
1963	H.R.ROKEBY-JOHNSON		10
1964	B.H.BUCKLEY		8

Founders' Cup

SINGLES

Year	Name		Handicap
1965	H.R.ROKEBY - JOHNSON	Handicap	9
1966	C.P.C.DONALD		12
1967	D.H.R.HOLLAND		5
1968	W.T.McEWAN		5
1969	B.W.MELBOURN		11
1970	W.T.McEWAN		5
1971	E.D.S.ALDRICH - BLAKE		9
1972	Capt. C.B.Q.WALLACE		2
1973	D.H.R.HOLLAND		3
1974	C.J.BOGGON		8
1975	B.CRITCHLEY		1
1976	D.H.R.HOLLAND		4
1977	D.L.B.LANE		5
1978	Col. J.M.CUTLER		11
1979	R.M.GAMBLE		11
1980	R.H.G.SHARP		4
1981	V.M.SHAW		9
1982	R.M.GAMBLE		8
1983	A.D.H.BIGGINS		4
1984	M.W.H.TRICKETT		12
1985	R.P.LAWSON		8
1986	R.P.LAWSON		6
1987	N. J. LINDESAY-BETHUNE		9
1988	J.A.COX		7
1989	J.H.R.KELLOCK		3
1990	M.H.DIXON		2
1991	N.J.LINDESAY- BETHUNE		7
1992	J.B.O'C.CRAVEN		6
1993	A.J.HOWARD		4
1994	A.R.GUEST GORNALL		11
1995	A.D.H.BIGGINS		5
1996	J.G.SUTHERLAND PILCH		5
1997	G.E.STIMPSON		7
1998	R.F.D.GUEST GORNALL		6
1999	T.J.C.JENKINS		4

Founders' Cup

FOURSOMES

1902	B.E.CAMMELL (7) and J.WATERER (7).
1903	E.A.SMIRKE (Scr.) and E.W.WATERER (5).
1904	A.TINDAL-ATKINSON (4) and J.TINDAL-ATKINSON (5).
1905	C.C.LINGEN (Scr.) and J WATERER (5).
1906	GORDON CAMPBELL (16) and J.F.ANDERSON (14).
1907	S.W.LAWRENCE (10) and J.S.SKIDMORE (12).
1908	E.A.SMIRKE (+2) and E.W.WATERER (3).
1909	G.H.BURGES (10) and J.M.OLDHAM (9).
1910	E.HORACE HOLME (Scr.) and G.H.RAW (12).
1911	Col. C.C.ELLIS (9) and A.P.LANGTON (7).
1912	H.M.CANNON (9) and N.F.HUNTER (+3).
1913	H M CANNON (7) and N.F.HUNTER (+3).
1919	G.N.PHARAZYN (3) and E.DONNER (4).
1920	E.R.CAMPBELL (+1) and M.STONOR (7).
1921	E.R.CAMPBELL (+2) and M.STONOR (7).
1922	Capt. R.H.JOBSON (1) and A.F.EVANS (18).
1923	P.Q.REISS (4) and R.L.TINSLEY (5).
1924	E.CAMERON (12) and D.G.ISAACS (7).
1925	F.L.RANKIN (1) and PAUL AZBILL (3).
1926	F.L.RANKIN (1) and PAUL AZBILL (2).
1927	C.D.GRAY (Scr) and J.I.PAINE (2).
1928	R.H.de MONTMORENCY (+1) and F.S.A.BAKER (2).
1929	R.H.ANKETELL (8) and Major H.RUSSELL (4).
1930	D.H.KYLE (+2) and Capt. G.E.HAWKINS M.C. (2).
1931	J.GODDARD (10) and Major C.L.B.FRASER (6).
1932	R.H.COBBOLD (2) and G.E.MONKLAND (8).
1933	J.H.MANSFIELD (9) and Major A.C.McLACHLAN (7).
1934	W.ROSS-SMITH (13) and C.E.BEDFORD (15).
1935	N.C.SELWAY (+1) and J.H.MANSFIELD (7).
1936	Capt. G.E.HAWKINS (Scr.) and K.A.S.MORRICE (1).
1937	E.C.SEWARD (6) and L.S.FALK (7).
1938	L.G.CRAWLEY (+2) and P.H.MITCHELL (16).
1946	J.G.HANSON-LAWSON (Scr.) and V. LEMIEUX (12).
1947	T.E.CUNNINGHAM (4) and C.R.T.CUNNINGHAM (4).
1948	F.W.RICARDO (Scr.) and D.R.FOSTER (3).
1949	W.D.BISHOP (3) and D.L.PARTINGTON (5).
1950	C.W.ROBERTS (12) and C.A.MATON (8).
1951	J.GRIMDITCH (6) and C.REEVES (12).
1952	P.CHETTLE (12) and M.STOOP (7).
1953	A.N.BEACH (12) and P.ILLINGWORTH (7).
1954	I.M.PARKER (15) and A.C.SNOWDEN (13).
1955	J.HAWK (5) and T. LONGDON (9).
1956	A.O.BRIDGMAN (7) and H.D.WINKWORTH (19).
1957	P.J.OPPENHEIMER (9) and P.R.JEANTY (11).
1958	A.C.SNOWDEN (11) and B.W.WARNER (9).
1959	Major W.D.HENDERSON (Scr.) and A.ABELES (4).
1960	Col. G.S.K.MAYDON (4) and S.PLEYDELL-BOUVERIE (16).
1961	R.HUNTER (2) and B.CRITCHLEY (2).
1962	P.S.CLARK (3) and N.ROYDS (4).
1963	J.R.EARL (3) and P.CHETTLE (8).
1964	D.W.V.BENNETT (5) and R.J.G.SHAW (9).
1965	H.R.ROKEBY-JOHNSON (8) and D.H.R.HOLLAND (3).

Founders' Cup

FOURSOMES

1966	J.L.McCLUE (1) and R.A.P.KING (14).
1967	J.R.EARL (3) and D.H.R.HOLLAND(3).
1968	C.T.WALLIS (12) and B.W.MELBOURN (11).
1969	I.CALDWELL (2) and R.L.WADDINGTON (9).
1970	P.FRANCIS (18) and R.L.M.MORRIS (10).
1971	W.G.A.CLEGG (4) and S.C.S.MARTYN (13).
1972	Capt. F.B.LLOYD R.N. (14) and Capt. A.F.BLACK R.N.(8).
1973	J.C.DAVIES (+2) and J.R.EARL (6).
1974	The Hon. P.PAKENHAM (8). and J.C.MATHEW (12).
1975	N.C.ROYDS (6) and A.N.G.ROYDS (5).
1976	Dr. H.U.S.McMICHEN (2) and B.CAREY (2).
1977	C.R.DIMPFL (9) and C.P.C.DONALD (7).
1978	J.H.WILKINSON (4) and P.A.C.MACONIE (13).
1979	D.B.MILLER (9) and G.B.YOUNG (6).
1980	R.H.G.SHARP (5) and J.K.TULLIS (4).
1981	R.L.M.MORRIS (7) and R.H.BUXTON (10).
1982	R.H.THOMPSON (4) and R.M.GAMBLE (6).
1983	S.C.S.MARTYN (5) and J.S.W.HUNT (12).
1984	H.C.A.ROWE (8) and The Hon. R.FORTE (16).
1985	D.H.R.HOLLAND (5) and R.C.SEWARD (5).
1986	M.H.DIXON (3) and R.W.WALKER (9).
1987	J.A.COX (7) and R.J.G.HURST (4).
1988	D.A.O.DAVIES (8) and M.D.M.DAVIES (15).
1989	A.C.D.INGLEBY-MACKENZIE(11) and M.A.C.BUCKLEY(17).
1990	G.B.YOUNG (8) and R.D.K.YOUNG (8)
1991	S.C.N.BAGULEY (5) and T.J.C.JENKINS(5)
1992	J.G.JERMINE (Scr.) and P.F.GARNER (2)
1993	J.A.COX (6) and S.P.B.DENEHY (6)
1994	B.R.B.CARRICK (4) and M.C.J.NICHOLAS (12)
1995	S.C.N.BAGULEY (3) and Dr. C.J.LAWSON BAKER (9)
1996	J.B.O'C.CRAVEN (6) and M.A.C.BUCKLEY (16)
1997	S.C.N.BAGULEY (3) and Dr.C.J.LAWSON BAKER(9)
1998	J.A.D.WYKE (5) and A.P.D.WYKE (9)
1999	D.C.N.LONGMUIR (1) and D.Y.DAVIES (6)

Scratch Match Play Championship.

Year	Winner	Year	Winner	Year	Winner
1968	I.CALDWELL.	1980	K.S.GALLON.	1992	J.G.JERMINE.
1969	J.K.TULLIS.	1981	M.C.HUGHESDON.	1993	C.B.MANSON.
1970	R.HUNTER.	1982	A.D.H.BIGGINS.	1994	M.C.HUGHESDON.
1971	M.G.KING.	1983	M.H.DIXON.	1995	J.G.JERMINE.
1972	M.G.KING.	1984	I.M.STUNGO.	1996	M.L.AUBREY-FLETCHER
1973	M.G.KING.	1985	J.I.MARQUEZ.		
1974	M.C.HUGHESDON.	1986	A.J.HOWARD.	1997	M.L.AUBREY-FLETCHER
1975	J.C.DAVIES.	1987	P.D.M.CARR.		
1976	E.R.DEXTER.	1988	M.C.HUGHESDON.	1998	J.H.R.KELLOCK
1977	J.C.DAVIES.	1989	J.G.JERMINE.	1999	I.M.STUNGO
1978	N.de BRITO e CUNHA.	1990	P.D.M.CARR.		
1979	J.C.DAVIES.	1991	P.F.GARNER		

Longman Cup

Year	Name	Score		Year	Name	Score
1911	C. J. BURNUP	78+76·154		1984	M. H. DIXON	75+79·154
1912	H. E. TAYLOR	73+75·148		1985	M. C. HUGHESDON	71+72·143
1913	H. E. TAYLOR	78+81·159		1986	A. J. HOWARD	74+69·143
1919	The Hon. R. COKE	84+79·163		1987	M. C. HUGHESDON	77+66·143
1920	D. GRANT	79+78·157		1988	J. H. R. KELLOCK	77+68·145
1921	D. GRANT	75+76·151		1989	J. H. R. KELLOCK	77+70·147
1922	Col. H. E. HAMBRO	76+80·156		1990	M. H. DIXON	74+71·145
1923	E. R. CAMPBELL	74+76·150		1991	P. D. M. CARR	72+76·148
1924	Capt. R. H. JOBSON	73+75·148		1992	M. C. HUGHESDON	75+70·145
1925	S. K. THORBURN	74+78·152		1993	M. C. HUGHESDON	71+72·143
1926	H. GARDINER-HILL 76+73 Capt. R. H. JOBSON 74+75 ·149			1994	P. D. M. CARR	73+72·145
1927	Capt. R. H. JOBSON	78+72·150		1995	S. C. N. BAGULEY	75+73·148
1928	H. GARDINER-HILL 82+75 J. I. PAINE 83+74 ·157			1996	J. H. R. KELLOCK	76+72·148
1929	S. K. THORBURN	78+76·154		1997	J. H. R. KELLOCK	75+72·147
1930	D. H. KYLE	72+71·143		1998	M. DEVETTA	73+74·147
1931	D. H. KYLE	75+74·149		1999	R. CALDWELL	75+70·145
1932	R. HARTLEY	70+75·145				
1933	D. H. KYLE	76+73·149				
1934	D. H. KYLE	71+75·146				
1935	R. HARTLEY	75+72·147				
1936	T. E. CUNNINGHAM	76+71·147				
1937	T. A. BOURN	72+71·143				
1938	L. G. CRAWLEY	70+71·141				
1947	L. G. CRAWLEY	73+69·142				
1948	L. G. CRAWLEY	75+69·144				
1949	A. A. McNAIR	79+72·151				
1950	L. G. CRAWLEY	71+72·143				
1951	G. H. MICKLEM	73+71·144				
1952	P. F. McDONALD	73+74·147				
1953	J. W. FOLEY-BRICKLEY	75+76·151				
1954	P. W. G. NEEDHAM	76+75·151				
1955	G. H. MICKLEM	75+70·145				
1956	G. H. MICKLEM	72+72·144				
1957	G. T. DUNCAN	71+68·139				
1958	D. W. FRAME	73+72·145				
1959	D. H. R. HOLLAND	76+74·150				
1960	D. W. FRAME	71+76·147				
1961	M. D. DAWSON	72+78·150				
1962	I. CALDWELL	71+74·145				
1963	B. CRITCHLEY	73+75·148				
1964	I. CALDWELL	70+73·143				
1965	J. K. TULLIS	74+72·146				
1966	D. A. C. MARR	73+72·145				
1967	R. HUNTER	75+68·143				
1968	I. CALDWELL	75+76·151				
1969	I. CALDWELL	75+73·148				
1970	R. HUNTER	70+68·138				
1971	R. HUNTER	70+77·147				
1972	R. HUNTER	73+75·148				
1973	J. L. McCLUE	74+75·149				
1974	Major C. B. Q. WALLACE	71+80·151				
1975	M. C. HUGHESDON	75+72·147				
1976	D. H. R. HOLLAND	78+74·152				
1977	M. H. DIXON	78+72·150				
1978	J. C. DAVIES	72+70·142				
1979	A. R. KERR	72+76·148				
1980	J. C. DAVIES	75+70·145				
1981	M. H. DIXON	71+74·145				
1982	M. DEVETTA	78+72·150				
1983	D. H. R. HOLLAND	75+79·154				

Connaught Cup

Year	Name	Score		Year	Name	Score
1911	C. J. BURNUP	154+1·155		1986	H. C. A. ROWE	65+69·134
1912	H. E. TAYLOR	148+6·154		1987	J. G. SUTHERLAND PILCH	74+63·137
1913	H. E. TAYLOR	159+6·165		1988	T. H. ST. JOHN	60·71·131
1919	Hon. R. COKE	163-5·158		1989	T. J. C. JENKINS	66+71·137
1920	D. GRANT	157+4·161		1990	T. H. HARKER	70+68·138
1921	D. GRANT	151+4·155		1991	D. H. R. HOLLAND	72·67·139
1922	Col. H. E. HAMBRO	156+1·157		1992	A. T. BORTHWICK	62·66·128
1923	E. R. CAMPBELL	150+2·152		1993	J. N. KANAAN	66·71·137
1924	Capt. R. H. JOBSON	148+2·150		1994	T. J. C. JENKINS	65+70·135
1925	P. Q. REISS	161-8·153		1995	S. CHILTON	74·64·138
1926	H. GARDINER-HILL	149 Scr149		1996	A. D. H. BIGGINS	71·71·142
1927	Capt. R. H. JOBSON	150+2·152		1997	I. A. R. MURRAY	66·71·137
1928	J. I. PAINE	157-2·155		1998	N. R. A. TRICKEY	68+70·138
1929	Sir. THOMAS BARNES	165·10·155		1999	J. A. D. WYKE	65·71·136
1930	D. H. KYLE	143+3·146				
1931	R. H. ANKETELL	162-11·151				
1932	H. WATSON	168-17·151				
1933	G. A. R. KON	150-13·137				
1934	Sir ROBERT McLEAN	150-3·147				
1935	F. L. RANKIN	148-2·146				
1936	T. E. CUNNINGHAM	147-4·143				
1937	A. H. READ	148-4·144				
1938	L. G. CRAWLEY	141+4·145				
1947	L. G. CRAWLEY	142+4·146				
1948	P. W. G NEEDHAM	151-5·146				
1949	V. LEMIEUX	155-15·140				
1950	R. D. FORBES WATSON	153-8·145				
1951	A. R. EVERETT	167-24·143				
1952	Lt.Col. G. S. K. MAYDON	155-12·143				
1953	M. H. MEDWIN	164·20·144				
1954	G. DOBSON	166·24·142				
1955	R. W. KREFTING	147-6·141				
1956	N. ROYDS	157-17·140				
1957	G. T. DUNCAN	139 Scr 139				
1958	D. H. R. HOLLAND	148-4·144				
1959	E. W. T. MOSSELMANS	72+71·143				
1960	Capt. F. B. LLOYD, R.N.	73+71·144				
1961	L. H. MERTON	73+76·149				
1962	I. CALDWELL	71+74·145				
1963	J. G. HANSON-LAWSON	71+73·144				
1964	R. O. STEVENSON	71+71·142				
1965	D. W. V. BENNETT	70+71·141				
1966	J. W. HUMPHRIES	71+68·139				
1967	G. P. H. HOGAN-HEARN	69+71·140				
1968	J. ff CHURCHILL	75+72·147				
1969	P. G. M. WILSON	76+68·144				
1970	J. GARRELS	74+65·139				
1971	P. FRANCIS	72+66·138				
1972	J. F. WHITFIELD	76+74·150				
1973	C. R. BURN	70+76·146				
1974	R. C. SEWARD	64+78·142				
1975	T. V. BOARDMAN III	73+66·139				
1976	A. W. THOMPSON	68+69·137				
1977	R. M. GAMBLE	74+68·142				
1978	A. C. N. FERGUSON	74+68·142				
1979	A. C. N. FERGUSON	72+70·142				
1980	H. R. HOLLAND	74+69·143				
1981	I. CALDWELL	71+66·137				
1982	M. LIGHTWOOD	69+71·140				
1983	D. H. R. HOLLAND	70+65·135				
1984	R. D. BENZIE	71+64·135				
1985	N. LINDESAY-BETHUNE	68+64·132				

John Langley Cup

		New	Old	
1992	J.H.R.KELLOCK	72	71	143
1993	J.J.CARR	73	69	142
1994	P.D.M.CARR	72	73	145
1995	J.H.R.KELLOCK	72	68	140
1996	M.L.AUBREY-FLETCHER	70	73	143
1997	C.B.MANSON	73	73	146
1998	J.G.JERMINE	80	66	146
1999	S.J.STILWELL	72	65	137

Gordon Campbell Cup

1924	A.F. EVANS	2 up		1993	J.J.CARR	6 up
1925	N. LINGEN-BARKER	2 up		1994	J.N.KANAAN	7 up
1926	M.R. PHILIPSON	2 up		1995	C.C.LANE	4 up
1927	C.J. BURNUP	2 up		1996	J.K.TULLIS	4 up
1928	S.H. DAY	2 up		1997	S.O.GREEN-WILKINSON	3up
1929	C. MARTYN	3 up		1998	A.J.DAVIS	3up
1930	L.G. CRAWLEY	4 up		1999	Sir JOHN ROBB	2up
1931	R.B. FOSTER	4 up				
1932	J.H. RAMSDEN	4 up				
1933	Major J.H.ANDERSON	2 up				
1934	W.D. HOOPER	3 up				
1935	R.H. ANKETELL	1 up				
1936	Lt.Col. R.D. MILNER	3 up				
1937	PUTNAM EATON	2 up				
1938	M.J. SMYTH	5 up				
1939	R. BYASS	4 up				
1947	A. McNAIR	3 up				
1948	Col.N.IRELAND-SMITH	3 up				
1949	Col.N.IRELAND-SMITH	5 up				
1950	P.W.G.NEEDHAM	4 up				
1951	Col.N.IRELAND-SMITH	8 up				
1952	M.MEDWIN	6 up				
1953	Col.H.F.HEYWOOD	5 up				
1954	T.V. BOARDMAN	2 up				
1955	M.G.WARDLAW	2 up				
1956	J.G.NEEDHAM	5 up				
1957	Major T.H.GLADSTONE	4 up				
1958	Lt.Cdr.A.C.R.FANE,R.N.	6 up				
1959	B.H.BUCKLEY	2 up				
1960	G.R.KEENE	3 up				
1961	C.M.MOSSELMANS	4 up				
1962	A.N.BEACH	4 up				
1963	C.E.PARNELL	4 up				
1964	S.PLEYDELL-BOUVERIE	2 up				
1965	R.HUNTER	6 up				
1966	J.P. STEWART	7 up				
1967	A.G.BENZIE	7 up				
1968	G.P. H.HOGAN-HERN	5 up				
1969	Capt.A.F BLACK,DSC.,R.N	3 up				
1970	J.C.GARRELS	4 up				
1971	C.A.DOHERTY	9 up				
1972	B.D.L.JACOBS	4 up				
1973	P.A.CHAPPELL	5 up				
1974	Capt.B.E.T.GUBBINS	5 up				
1975	W.J.MARTIN	6 up				
1976	R.C.NELSON	5 up				
1977	B.S.KENT	3 up				
1978	W.G.LOCKEY	7 up				
1979	P.J.P. DONALD	7 up				
1980	E.H.R.FANE	7 up				
1981	P.J.P. DONALD	7 up				
1982	F.HADID	6 up				
1983	D.H.R.HOLLAND	5 up				
1984	R.N.SINGER	5 up				
1985	D.J.CONRAN	7 up				
1986	J.D.I.COWPER	9 up				
1987	J.D.I.COWPER	6 up				
1988	C.MARTYN	7 up				
1989	A.D.H.BIGGINS	7 up				
1990	T.F.St JOHN	10up				
1991	Sir PETER HOLMES	8 up				
1992	Dr.H.U.S.McMICHEN	7 up				

Dunedin Cup

Year	Name	Score
1923	Capt. K. THORBURN, M.C.	78-1-77
1924	T. M. McKENNA	79-12-67
1925	C. R. BLANDFORD	80-4-76
1926	H. J. COXHEAD	73-2-71
1927	M. STONER	85-11-74
1928	G. A. R. KON	78-6-72
1929	C. H. MEARS	88-12-76
1930	L. G. CRAWLEY	73 Scr 73
1931	D. H. KYLE	69+2-71
1932	A. E. EDWARD	79-8-71
1933	Col. R. D. MILNER	80-10-70
1934	Major G. H. ANDERSON	80-10-70
1935	G. M. NIALL	72-5-67
1936	F. L. RANKIN	77 Scr 77
1937	W. R. BERRY	83-12 71
1938	S. G. SILLEM	75-4-71
1951	D. M. CLAYTON	83-12-71
1952	R. MARRIOTT	76-8-68
1953	T. L. R. HOLLAND	83-13-70
1954	D. DOULTON	82-14-68
1955	J. G. HANSON LAWSON	76-7-69
1956	G. S. STONE	87-19-68
1957	G. A. WOLSEY	86-15-71
1958	P. OPPENHEIMER	77-8-69
1959	P. B. MANSON	84-13-71
1960	J. R. BOARDMAN	77-5-72
1961	J. L. McCLUE	68 Scr 68
1962	J. G. HANSON-LAWSON	79-9-70
1963	J. A. T. GUEST	80-7-73
1964	E. W. HUNNISETTE	85-14-71
1965	D. H. R. HOLLAND	74-3-71
1966	C. R. NATER	85-16-69
1967	C. MURRAY-BROWN	84-14-70
1968	M. J. G. KNOX	78-8-70
1969	C. L. ELLIOTT	79-8-71
1970	G. B. YOUNG	78-6-72
1971	S. CONNERY	82-13-69
1972	G. A. ELLIOT	79-9-70
1973	J. R. BOARDMAN	72-5-67
1974	R. C. NELSON	82-11-71
1975	J. R. BOARDMAN	70-4-66
1976	D. G. E. BENZIE	84-16-68
1977	Col. J. M. CUTLER	79-11-68
1978	Dr. P. G. O. KAMILL	81-12-69
1979	L. R. H. GRACEY	77-4-73
1980	L. R. H. GRACEY	72-4-68
1981	D. A. O. DAVIES	77-6-71
1982	P. B. MANSON	83-10-73
1983	D. M. JONES	79-11-68
1984	R. M. L. HUMPHREYS	79-12-67
1985	G. B. YOUNG	77-8-69
1986	D. J. G. ROYDS	77-6-71
1987	C. S. MARTYN	78-6-72
1988	P. E. HAYWARD	74-8-66
1989	R. D. K. YOUNG	77-8-69
1990	T. H. HARKER	74-9-65
1991	Dr. C. J. LAWSON BAKER	78-10-68
1992	M. DEVETTA	68-2-66
1993	P. HALE	77-5-72
1994	J. G. SUTHERLAND PILCH	74-5-69
1995	R. D. K. YOUNG	75-7-68
1996	A. C. AYLWIN	80-9-71
1997	M. C. HUGHESDON	69-1-68
1998	J. D. I. COWPER	83-15-68
1999	C. McCLEAN	80-11-69

Dormy House Shield

1951	S. G. SILLEM
1952	P. W. G. NEEDHAM
1953	A. D. R. HOLLAND
1954	R. A. GOLD
1955	I. CALDWELL
1956	H. R. ROKEBY-JOHNSON
1957	D. ALDRICH-BLAKE
1958	D. H. R. HOLLAND
1959	D. W. FRAME
1960	C. ff. CHURCHILL
1962	R. D. A. GALBRAITH
1963	J. P. GOLD
1964	R. H. BUXTON
1965	W. C. HUTCHINS
1966	A. G. BENZIE
1967	J. W. HUMPHRIES
1968	A. G. BENZIE
1969	R. H. BUXTON
1970	B. D. L. JACOBS
1971	S. A. McNAIR
1972	C. B. Q. WALLACE
1973	J. R. BOARDMAN
1974	P. W. GOULD
1975	NO COMPETITION
1976	C. R. DIMPFL
1977	W. LAVOIE
1978	C. P. C. DONALD
1979	H. R. HOLLAND
1980	R. S. GUBBINS
1981	N. J. R. BURN
1982	N. J. R. BURN
1983	E. R. DEXTER
1984	I. M. STUNGO
1985	E. R. DEXTER
1986	J. G. SUTHERLAND PILCH
1987	J. M. McMILLAN
1988	J. B. HODGSON
1989	N. J. LINDESAY-BETHUNE
1990	Dr. H. U. S. McMICHEN
1991	P. SEDGWICK
1992	J. R. COLLIN
1993	C. C. LANE
1994	J. R. COLLIN
1995	J. K. TULLIS
1996	J. K. TULLIS
1997	M. H. DIXON
1998	J. M. McMILLAN
1999	J. A. D. WYKE

Sillem Bowls

1972	W. D. BISHOP Wing Cdr. C. N. McLOUGHLIN
1973	J. C. DEEKS C. L. ELLIOTT
1974	E. HAMILTON-HILL Capt. D. VINCENT-JONES, R.N.
1975	NO COMPETITION
1976	A. R. MASON A. VAN ZWANENBERG
1977	A. A. McNAIR Wing Cdr. C. N. McLOUGHLIN
1978	A. A. McNAIR Wing Cdr. C. N. McLOUGHLIN
1979	J. W. HUMPHRIES J. C. DEEKS
1980	W. CHASSELS J. D. I. COWPER
1981	S. K. PRESTIGE D. A. WICKINS
1982	W. CHASSELS J. D. I. COWPER
1983	W. CHASSELS J. D. I. COWPER
1984	W. CHASSELS J. D. I. COWPER
1985	Dr. E. O. WALWYN-JONES A. J. HUGHES
1986	D. B. MILLER G. B. YOUNG
1987	J. D. I. COWPER V. Adm. R. F. SCHOULTZ (U.S.N.)
1988	Maj. A. K. BARLOW G. H. DIXON
1988	T. E. D. HARKER D. A. O. DAVIES
1989	D. A. O. DAVIES T. E. D. HARKER
1990	A. C. R. FANE D. P. A. COX
1991	A. C. R. FANE D. P. A. COX
1992	W. T. CAMPBELL L. GRACEY
1993	T. F. StJOHN R. ANDRESEN
1994	T. F. StJOHN R. ANDRESEN
1995	T. F. StJOHN R. ANDRESEN
1996	D. B. COBB J. M. C. PUCKRIDGE
1997	J. D. I. COWPER I. CALDWELL
1998	B. E. STURGESS D. M. BERLIAND
1999	J. C. MARLEY J. B. HODGSON

Lady Captains

1953	Mrs	J. D. A. LANGLEY
1954	Mrs	A. C. CRITCHLEY
1955	Mrs	J. ANDREWS
1956	Mrs	J. ANDREWS
1957	Mrs	W. G. M. PRICE
1958	Mrs	G. S. STONE
1959	Mrs	J. WILSON
1960	Mrs	R. B. HUNTER
1961	Mrs	M. V. ARNELL
1962	Mrs	C. MURRAY BROWN
1963	Mrs	A. C. SNOWDEN
1964	Mrs	C. ABRAHAMS
1965	Mrs	A. A. VAN ZWANENBERG
1966	Mrs	S. M. LE BAS
1967	Mrs	G. H. DIXON
1968	Mrs	A. HANBURY
1969	The Lady	ROSEMARY MUIR
1970	Mrs	G. E. GOODHEW
1971	Mrs	J. B. L. JACOBS
1972	Mrs	J. B. L. JACOBS
1973	Mrs	G. H. DUNBAR. C.B.E.
1974	Mrs	C. DUGAN-CHAPMAN
1975	Mrs	B. T. WINGFIELD
1976	Mrs	J. C. MATHEW
1977	Lady	BROWN
1978	Mrs	D. A. BRAITHWAITE
1979	Mrs	D. H. R. HOLLAND
1980	Mrs	J. R. BOARDMAN
1981	Mrs	J. K. TULLIS
1982	Mrs	A. D. McCORMICK
1983	Mrs	M. D. PETCH
1984	Mrs	I. CALDWELL
1985	Mrs	M. W. T. LEATHAM
1986	Mrs	A. W. N. GARRATT
1987	Mrs	N. P. THOMAS
1988	Mrs	A. C. R. FANE
1989	Mrs	G. CHASE GARDENER
1990	Mrs	T. E. D. HARKER
1991	Mrs	D. P. C. BEARD
1992	Mrs	D. S. A. PEARCE

1993	Mrs	M. C. HUGHESDON
1994	Mrs	E. R. DALE-HARRIS
1995	Mrs	L. M. HUNTER
1996	Mrs	P. MELBYE HOWARD
1997	Mrs	C. L. A. WALPOLE
1998	Mrs	E. G. PITHERS
1999	Mrs	M. C. JONES

Critchley Salver

1982	Miss. H.REID
1983	Miss. K.DOUGLAS
1984	Mrs. J.E.BAYMAN
1985	Mrs. J.E.BAYMAN
1986	Mrs. K.WOOLDRIDGE
1987	Miss. P.M.JOHNSON
1988	Miss. S.P.MOORCRAFT
	Mrs. J.E.BAYMAN
	Miss. J.WADE
1989	Miss. L.FLETCHER
1990	Miss. C.HOURIHANE
1991	Miss. N.L.BUXTON
1992	Mrs. C.CALDWELL
1993	Mrs. C.G.WATSON
1994	Mrs. S.LAMBERT
	Miss. K.SPEAK
1995	Miss. K.TEBBET
	Mrs. A.UZIELLI
1996	Miss. S.GALLAGHER
1997	Miss. L.WALTERS
1998	Miss. L.WALTERS
1999	Miss. L.CTUPHOLME

Sunningdale Foursomes

1934	Miss D. FISHWICK & E. NOEL LAYTON
1935	Miss J. WETHERED & J.S.F. MORRISON
1936	Miss J. WETHERED & J.S.F. MORRISON
1937	A.S. ANDERSON & D.J. REES
1938	Miss P. BARTON & A. PADGHAM
1939	C. RISSIK & E.W.H. KENYON
1948	Miss W. MORGAN & S. KING
1949	R.G. FRENCH & S.S. FIELD
1950	M. FAULKNER & J. KNIPE
1951	Miss J. DONALD & T. HALIBURTON
1952	P.F. SCRUTTON & A. WATERS
1953	Miss J. DONALD & T. HALIBURTON
1954	P.F. SCRUTTON & A. WATERS
1955	W.R. SHARP & S.S. SCOTT
1956	G. KNIPE & D. SMALLDON
1957	B. HUGGETT & R. WHITEHEAD
1958	Miss J. DONALD & P. ALLISS
1959	M.F. BONALLACK & D.N. SEWELL
1960	Miss B. McCORKINDALE & M.J. MOIR
1961	Mrs J. ANDERSON & P. ALLISS
1962	N. COLES & R. WHITEHEAD
1963	L. PLATTS & D. SNELL
1964	B. CRITCHLEY & R. HUNTER
1965	Mrs A.D. SPEARMAN & T. FISHER
1966	R.R.W. DAVENPORT & A.N. WALKER
1967	N. COLES & K. WARREN
1968	J.C. DAVIES & W. HUMPHREYS
1969	P.J. BENKA & P. OOSTERHUIS
1970	Miss A. WILLARD & R.J. BARRELL
1971	A. BIRD & H. FLATMAN
1972	J.C. DAVIES & M.G. KING
1973	J.A. PUTT & Miss M. EVERARD
1974	C. CLARK & P. BUTLER
1975	ABANDONED — SNOW
1976	C. CLARK & M.C. HUGHESDON
1977	G.M. HUNT & D. MATTHEW
1978	A. CAYGILL & Miss J.A. GREENHALGH
1979	G. WILL & R. CHAPMAN
1980	N. COLES & D. McCLELLAND
1981	A. LYDDON & G. BRAND
1982	Miss M. WALKER & Miss C. LANGFORD

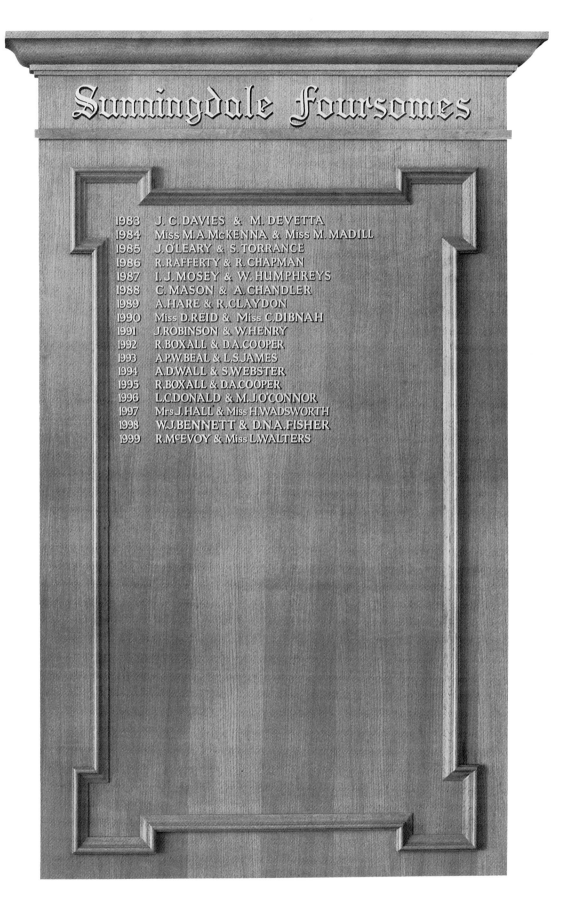

Sunningdale Foursomes

1983	J. C. DAVIES & M. DEVETTA
1984	Miss M.A.McKENNA & Miss M. MADILL
1985	J. O'LEARY & S. TORRANCE
1986	R. RAFFERTY & R. CHAPMAN
1987	I. J. MOSEY & W. HUMPHREYS
1988	C. MASON & A. CHANDLER
1989	A. HARE & R. CLAYDON
1990	Miss D. REID & Miss C. DIBNAH
1991	J. ROBINSON & W. HENRY
1992	R. BOXALL & D.A. COOPER
1993	A.P.W. BEAL & L.S. JAMES
1994	A.D. WALL & S. WEBSTER
1995	R. BOXALL & D.A. COOPER
1996	L.C. DONALD & M.J. O'CONNOR
1997	Mrs J. HALL & Miss H. WADSWORTH
1998	W.J. BENNETT & D.N.A. FISHER
1999	R. McEVOY & Miss L. WALTERS

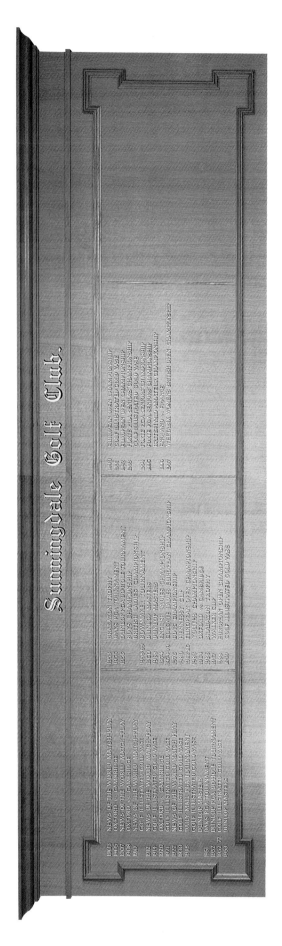

Some of the Club Trophies
- Founders Singles and Foursomes Cups at centre rear.

Some of the Ladies Trophies
- the Colgate Cup at centre rear.

Secretaries of the Club

1900-01	Hon. Montague Erskine - Hon. Secretary
1901-11	H.S. Colt
1911-13	H.S. Colt & K. Greenway - Joint Secretaries
1913-16	Major N.F. Williams Re-joined the Army in 1914. Died 1916.
1914-16	H.S. Colt - Acting Secretary
1917-19	T.A. Roberts - Hon. Secretary
1919-33	F.P. LeMarchand
1933-40	Major G.G.M. Bennett
1940-46	J. Moir - Hon. Secretary
1946-50	G.G. Kirke
1950-60	B. Drew
1960-63	Commander L.A. Jeffrey O.B.E., R.N.
1964-69	Colonel R.E.S. Yeldham O.B.E.
1970-71	J.F. Whitfield - Hon. Secretary
1971-73	L. Haigh
1973-78	J.F. Whitfield - Club Director
1978-91	K. Almond
1991-	J.A.S. Zuill

Index

A

d'Abo G.L. *38*

Abrahams, Louisa (Lady Abrahams) *147*

Agate, Jeffrey *116, 117*

Albert, HH Prince of Schleswig Holstein *10, 15, 16, 17*

Aldrich-Blake A. de C. *134*

Aldrich-Blake E.D.S. *134*

Alfredsson, Helen *90*

Alliss, Peter *126*

Almond, Keith *50, 116*

Anketell R.H. *69*

Aoki, Isao *130*

Arthur, Jim *50*

B

Baguley, Sean *79*

Baird, Maurice *150*

Baker, F.S.A. *38, 39*

Barlow, P. *3*

Barnes, Brian *125*

Battell, Mr. *25*

Beamish, Wing Cdr. C.H. *119*

Beaufort, Lady Margaret of *1*

Beck, John *150*

Beharell, G.E. *38, 39*

Benedictine Nunnery of Broomhall *1*

Bennett, Bob *51*

Bennett, Major Guy *4, 30, 33, 59, 127*

Bentley, Harry *112, 137*

Biggins, Tony *53*

Bingham, Lawson *51*

Bingham, Michael *31, 33, 34*

Blackwell, E.B.H. *135*

Blair, David *114, 127*

Boardman, John *116, 117, 150*

Boardman, Mrs. Patsy *116, 117*

Bonallack, Michael *111, 116, 120, 125, 150*

Boomer, Percy *34, 36, 100*

Bourn, T. (Dale) *109, 136, 137*

Brabazon, Lord *152*

Bradley, Pat *90*

Braid, James *20, 23, 24, 34, 94, 97, 98, 99*

Bristowe, Gerald *133*

Brito e Cuna (Visconde de Pereira Machado) *138*

Brodie, Allan *119*

Broomhall Farm *1*

Bruen, James *109*

Bugler, Lyn *52*

Burgess, Michael *125*

Burton, Dick *101*

Butler, Peter *126*

C

Cafe Monico *1*

Caldwell, Mrs Carole *86, 147*

Caldwell, Ian *113, 114, 116, 118, 133, 134, 138, 153*

Campbell, E.R. *135*

Campbell, Sir Gordon *25*

Campbell, W.T. (Tommie) *138*

Carr, John *138*

Carr, Joe *111, 116, 120, 150, 153*

Carr, Philip *138*

Carr, R.J. (Roddy) *115, 138*

Challen, Charles *120*

Chapman, Bert *4, 152*

Chapman, Dick *118*

Charles, R.J. *128*

Cheney, Miss Joan *21*

Christie, Agatha *28*

Christie, Colonel A. *28*

Clark, Clive *48, 49, 111, 112, 119, 126*

Clark, D. *115*

Clarke, H.C. *3, 99*

Coles, Neil *125*

Collett, Glenna *83*

Collinson, Vernon *53*

Colt, H.S. *5, 12, 18, 20, 21, 22, 24, 25, 62, 65, 68, 107, 139, 149, 150, 152*

Coltart, T. *137*

Connaught, H.R.H. The Duke of *6*

Cornelius, Vivian *152*

Cotton, Henry *34, 100, 102*
Cowper, Mrs Joan *147*
Crawley, Leonard *21, 111, 112, 113, 118, 132, 133, 134, 136, 139*
Creasy, R. *3*
Critchley, Brigadier-General A.C. *36, 38, 83, 139*
Critchley, Bruce *111, 115, 125, 133, 134, 139*
Critchley, Mrs Diana *83, 147*
Cunningham, T.E. *38, 39*

D
Darwin, Bernard *55, 111, 135*
Davies, John *111, 115, 119, 125, 133, 134, 139*
Davies, David *116*
Davies, Derek *116, 139*
Davies, Laura *90*
Dawson, John *108*
Dawson, M.D. *140*
Deedes, Bill (Lord Deedes) *117*
Delacombe, Lucy *52*
Demaret, Jimmy *101*
Derby, Lord *127*
Devetta, Martin *140*
Dexter, Ted *134, 140*
Dimpfl, Bob *103*
Donald, Jean *125*
Donovan, Christopher *52*
Drew, Bernard *40, 49*
Drummond, Sergeant T. *52*
Dugan-Chapman, Charles *140*
Duncan, Colonel A.A. *140*
Duncan, George *140*

E
Elliott, Cecil *50, 116, 149*
Erskine, The Hon: Montague *4, 5*

F
Faldo, Nick *65, 130*
Faulkner, Max *124, 125*
Fiddian, E. *109*
Fisher, John: Bishop of Rochester *1*
Fishwick, Diana *83, 124*

Fleming, H. Gibson *38, 39*
Fletcher, James *53*
Flynn, Mickey *51*
Forest, John de (Count John de Bendern) *109, 111, 140*
Forte, the Hon: Rocco (Sir Rocco) *116*
Foster, David *103, 128*
Frame, David *115, 133, 140*
Francis, Craig *140*
Francis, Frank *140*
Furgol, Marty *103*

G
Gardiner-Hill, H. *135, 150*
Gardner, Robert *107*
Garner, P. *126, 141*
Gordon House *2*
Gourlay, Molly *83*
Govett, F.A. *24*
Grace, Dr. W.G. *137*
Gracey, Lionel *141*
Green, Peter *125*
Greenway, K. *12*
Griffiths, The Rt. Hon: Lord *150*
Griffiths, Miss Molly *21*
Grindrod, Murray *141*
Guest-Gornall, Richard *53*
Guilford, J.P. *111*

H
Haig, Field Marshal Earl *24*
Haigh, Lawrence *49*
Hale, Peter *53*
Haliburton, Tom *124*
Hall, E. Marshall K.C. *6*
Halstead, Mary *87*
Hambro, Angus *150*
Harker, Ted *116, 117, 150*
Harrison, Charles *141*
Hartley, Lister *111, 132, 134, 141*
Hartley, Rex *111, 132, 134, 141*
Henderson, Major Dalt *103*
Heppel, Mrs H.M. *21*
Herd, Alexander *34, 94*

Hewitt, Halford 152
Higuchi, Chako 129
Hilton, Harold 86, 87, 118
Hoare, David 141
Holderness, Ernest 107
Holland, David 141
Howard, A.J. 141
Howard, C. 3
Hughesdon, Michael 116, 126, 133, 142
Humphreys, Warren 125
Hunter, F. Mansfield 19, 24
Hunter, Norman F. 17, 18, 19, 24, 142
Hunter, Robin 119, 125, 132, 133, 142

J

Jeffrey, Commander L.A., R.N. 49
Jermine, J. 142
Jobson, Captain R.H. 132, 152
Jones, Bobby 26, 27, 30, 34, 111, 118, 122
Jones, Mervyn 50, 116
Jones, Rosie 90
Jubilee Course 30, 31, 32, 33

K

Kellock, Rupert 134
Kelly, Tim 151
King Edward VIII 30
King George V 30
King George VI 31, 35
King, Michael 115, 142
Kirkaldy, A. 97
Kirke, George 35, 40
Knocker, Chris 116
Kyle, Denis 111, 132, 136

L

Lane, Christopher 51
Langer, Bernhard 130
Langley, John 112, 113, 114, 118, 119, 133, 134, 142
Layton, Noel 83, 124
Lebert, Madame 22
Lees, Arthur 36, 40, 42, 47, 48, 99, 100, 101, 102, 103, 104, 105, 107

Leitch, Cecilia 86, 87
Le Marchand, F.P. 23, 30
Leuchars, Major-General Peter 53
Lindley, David 52
Lindsay, The Earl of 38
Lingen, C.C. 107, 132, 142
Lloyd, Captain F.B., R.N. 128
Locke, A.D. 128, 136
Lomas, D. 120
Longhurst, Henry 38, 40, 88, 152
Longman, Hubert H. 2
Lopez, Nancy 90, 129
de Lorenzi, Marie-Laure 90
Lound, C. 3
Lucan, Lord 47
Lucas, Wing Cdr. P.B. 38, 113, 143
Lunt, Michael 120

M

MacGillivray, Hugh 51
Maclean, Hugh 4, 11, 18, 26, 33, 95
Maclean, Jim 41, 51
Mangrum, Lloyd 101
Mathew, John QC 116, 117
Maugham, Somerset 152
Maxwell, Keith 49
McClue, Leslie 133, 143
McCready, S.M. (Max) 110, 113, 143
McEwan, Rab 151
McMichen, Dr. Hamish 143
McMillan, Jack 51
McNair, Andrew 118, 143
McNair, Stewart 143
Micklem, Gerald 50, 109, 113, 114, 116, 118, 133, 134, 143, 148, 149, 150
Millard, "Bunny" 96
Millard, P.C. 95, 96
Minoprio, Gloria 87, 88
Minoprio, John 87
Moir, James 33, 34, 35, 128
de Monmorency, R.H. 58, 118, 126
Morey, D. 114
Morrison, J.S.F. 70, 73, 118, 124, 143, 150, 152
Mullens, Ron 129
Munn, L. 109

N

Nagle, K.D.G. *128*
Neele, Miss Nancy *28*
Nelson, Byron *100*
New Course *24, 25, 26, 29, 30, 32, 34, 35, 36, 37, 38, 42, 43, 63-76*
Newnes, Sir George *96*
von Nida, Norman *100*
Nine Hole Course *76-78*
Norman, Greg *130*

O

O'Brian, Jim *8*
Oldham, J.M. *28*
Old Course *6, 25, 26, 30, 34, 36, 42, 43, 56-65*
Oliver, "Porky" *100, 101*
Onslow, Earl of *24, 42, 43, 65*
Ooi, Douglas *144*
Osborne, Chris *52*
Ouimet, Francis *111*

P

Paddock, H.D. Jr. *113, 114*
Padgham, Alf *124*
Park, William Jr. *2, 4, 55*
Pearman, Richard *144*
Perkins, T.P. *111*
Phillips, Van *120*
Pinero, Manuel *130*
Pitamber, Raj Kumar *144*
Player, Gary *120*
Pritchard, J. *3*
Puckridge, James *116*
Putt, John *144*

R

Rankin, Judy *90, 129*
Ransom, Henry *101*
Rattigan, Terence *152*
Ray, Ted *94, 96*
Rees, Dai *124*
Reeves, Harry *53*
Reeves, Vince *53*

Ricardo, Francis *144*
"Ridgemount" *1, 2*
Ridgemount Estate Company *1*
Ridgemount Working Men's Club *10, 28*
Rigden, W.J. *3*
Robb, James *107*
Roberts, G.A. *1, 35, 38*
Roberts, T.A. *v, 1, 2, 3, 4, 21, 35*
Roe, Ken *52*
Royds, Nicholas *47, 50, 116, 117, 150*

S

Scales, E.F. *28, 31*
Scott, Fred *53*
Scott, The Hon: Denys *95*
Scott, The Hon: Michael *109*
Scott, The Hon: Osmund *107, 132, 144*
Scrutton, Philip *114, 118, 125, 144*
Selway, N.C. *118*
Senior, Peter *130*
Sewell, Doug *125*
Shaw, Richard *152*
Sheridan, J. *11, 18, 20, 32, 34, 35, 41, 89*
Sherlock, J. *94, 97*
Siderowf, Dick *111*
Sillem, Stephen G. *38, 39, 66, 70, 76*
Simpson, Tom *30, 67, 68, 71*
Smirke, E.R. *107, 144*
Smith, E. *109*
Smith, General J.E. *127*
Smith, John *108, 109*
Smyth, N.J. *38*
Snead, Sam *101*
St. John's College *1, 11, 12, 35, 37, 40, 42, 43, 44*
Stavehall or Broomhall Waste *2*
Stilwell, Simon J. *65*
Storey, Eustace *107, 108, 111, 134, 145*
Stowe, Charlie *148*
Stranahan, Frank *110*
Streather, Bruce *145, 153*
Stungo, Ian *145*
Sunningdale Artisans Golf Club *28, 33, 36, 41, 117*
Sunningdale Heath Golf Club *12, 17, 24*

Sunningdale Ladies Golf Club *41, 82*
Sutherland Pilch, Jeremy *145*
Sweeney, Robert Jr. *109, 133, 145*

T
Tate, J.K. *119*
Taylor, H.E. *132*
Taylor, J.H. *20, 23, 94, 97, 98*
Thomas, Mrs Anita *116, 117*
Thomson, P.W. *128*
Thompson, Richard *116*
Thorburn, Major S.K. *118, 132, 136*
Titlarks Farm *1, 12*
Tolley, Cyril *59, 107, 108, 109, 111, 112, 134,*
      145, 150
Tullis, John *62, 116, 117, 145*
Turner, Archie *51*
Turner, Brian *51*
Turnesa, Willie *110*

V
Vardon, Harry *19, 20, 23, 97, 98, 99*
Vardon, Tom *92, 93, 94, 97, 99*
Villiers, E.E. *21*

W
Wales, HRH The Prince of *25, 29, 30, 150*
Wall, Anthony *53, 126, 145*
Wallace, Lt. Gen: Sir Christopher *146*
Ward, Charlie *101*
Washington, Sergeant George *6, 12*
Waters, A. *125*
Watt, Jimmie *48*
Webb, Karrie *90*
Webster, Steven *126*
Wethered, Joyce *89, 124, 152*
Wethered, R.H. *135*
White, Jack *3, 4, 7, 8, 11, 18, 20, 23, 27, 92, 93,*
      94, 96, 97, 98, 99
White, Ronnie *148*
Whitehead, Ross *125*
Whitfield, John *49, 50*
Wickins, David *47*
Wilkinson, John *53*

Williams, Dr. John *113*
Williams, Major N.F. *13, 17, 20*
Wilmot, Andrew *146*
Wolsey, Gordon *104*
Wolstenholme, Guy *114, 115, 119, 146*
Woodbridge, Cecil M. *3*
Woosnam, Ian *130*
Worsham, Lew *100*

Y
Yeldham, Colonel Ronnie *49*
York, HRH The Duke of *25, 30, 31, 150*
Young, Donna *129*
Young, Graham *116, 128*

Z
Zaharias, "Babe" *89*
Zuill, Stewart *50*